Eight Secrets to Highly Effective Parenting

Dr. Scott Turansky, D. Min.
and
Joanne Miller, RN, BSN

76 Hopatcong Dr. • Lawrenceville, NJ 08648
1-800-771-8334

First Paperback Printing: February 1996

Eight Secrets to Highly Effective Parenting
by Dr. Scott Turansky, D. Min., and Joanne Miller, RN, BSN

Published in Lawrenceville, New Jersey, by Effective Parenting, Inc.

Unless otherwise noted, Scripture quotations are from The Holy Bible, NEW INTERNATIONAL VERSION. Copyright © 1978 by the New York International Bible Society. Used by permission of Zondervan Bible Publishers.

The names of persons who have come to Effective Parenting for counseling have been changed to protect confidentiality.

Stories of the authors' children have been used by permission.

Effective Parenting is a nonprofit corporation committed to the communication of sound Biblical parenting principles through teaching, counseling and the publication of written, audio and video materials.

An audio cassette series, *"Eight Secrets to Highly Effective Parenting,"* is also available. To obtain a complete list of resources available from Effective Parenting or to have Scott Turansky and Joanne Miller come and present their material live, you may contact:

Effective Parenting
76 Hopatcong Dr.
Lawrenceville, NJ 08648
(800) 771-8334
(609) 771-8002
fax: (609) 771-8003

ISBN 1-888685-00-X

Library of Congress Catalog Card Number: 95-83085

Proofreading by Margaret Packard and Shirley Brode.

Cover design and interior illustrations by
Mike Kabbash and Mike DiFiori, iggybragg design, ltd.

—Dedication—

*This book is dedicated, first and above all,
to the glory of God.
And it is our prayer that many will find
the greatest secret of all—
Life in Jesus Christ.*

—With Special Thanks —

To my wife, Carrie, for her faithfulness to God and to me, and to our delightful children, Joshua, Melissa, Benjamin, Elizabeth and Megan, who have helped us test these secrets.

Scott Turansky

To my husband, Ed, for his unfailing support and encouragement which have been an invaluable contribution to this project, and to our wonderful boys, David and Timothy, whose energy and enthusiasm have inspired me to continue on.

Joanne Miller

**For your convenience
a form is included at
the back of this book
to order more books,
booklets, or tapes.**

Table of Contents

Eight Secrets

Introduction

"Okay, it's your turn," my[*] father said as he handed me the keys to the car for the first time. With feelings of excitement coupled with fear I slid into the driver's seat. I had spent many hours studying how to drive, memorizing speed limits, road signs, emergency procedures, hand signals and a myriad of other helpful information. I had observed others handle themselves in the driver's seat, watched movies about driving, and listened to lectures about the habits of good drivers. But now it was my turn. I remember putting my hands on the steering wheel and wondering, "What do I do now?" I learned that day that there's a big difference between studying how to drive and driving itself.

Parenting is a lot like that. It's one thing to study books on parenting where you find yourself nodding in agreement. Somehow, though, you end up wondering what to do when your four-year-old son has a

---

[*]Scott

tantrum in the grocery store or refuses to eat his dinner, or when your winsome daughter can't seem to keep her shoes on her feet for more than a few minutes at a time or your teenager responds to you with a disrespectful attitude. You begin to wonder if all that reading and studying about parenting did any good.

"What do I do now?" you often ask yourself. Raising children is one of the most challenging responsibilities and all parents find themselves frustrated from time to time.

Sometimes parents are confused because they just don't know what to do. They feel like the mother who saw her three-year-old son put a nickel in his mouth and swallow it. She immediately picked him up, turned him upside down and hit him on the back and he coughed up two dimes! Frantic, she called to the father outside. "Your son just swallowed a nickel and coughed up two dimes! What should I do?"

The father yelled back, "Keep feeding him nickels!"

Don't you wish solutions could be that easy?

Too often parents want instant answers for problems that took weeks or months to develop. Worthwhile solutions take work before the situation improves. Don't assume that things will eventually get better unless you are willing to embrace the solutions and make the necessary changes.

Life is demanding with pressures squeezing from every side. Parenting, though, requires a lifetime investment. It's not something one can just do during commercial breaks or while driving children to school.

But there is help available. This book explains and illustrates eight secrets which make parenting easier and more effective. Learning and applying these secrets will improve your parenting, and, in today's hectic world, some good ideas can sure help. These secrets are not a magic wand, though. They will require some work on your part.

In this book you will meet Craig and Marlene, parents just like any of us, struggling to respond to the day-to-day challenges of raising children. They've been married for nine years and have two children, Jennifer, age seven, and Danny, age four. You'll identify with Craig and Marlene as you see them wanting to guide their children toward mature behavior . . . but some days just trying to survive the afternoon. This book is divided into eight chapters, each one independent of the others. Although each secret is important, feel free to read and reread chapters that best meet your needs now.

Neither Craig nor Marlene have had any instruction in child rearing . . . but who has? They've picked up ideas along the way—some helpful, and others not so helpful. The questions they ask and the feelings they have will seem familiar to you. You are about to read the story of how one family learned some valuable secrets which made their parenting more effective and rewarding. These secrets work . . . and they'll work for you. So, find a comfortable chair, grab a hot drink and journey with Craig and Marlene on their adventure and . . . who knows . . . you, too, may learn some secrets that will change your life.

Secret One

The Secret To Prompt Obedience

"Everybody grab a bag," Marlene said as she turned the car into the driveway. She wished she could go grocery shopping alone but that meant either going at night or on the weekend. Having children along made the job more complicated.

"Well, at least we're home," Marlene thought as she parked the car. "One advantage of having children along is that they can help bring in the groceries." As she turned the car off, Marlene said, "Each of you find a bag you can carry."

"But Mom," said Jennifer, "I need to go to the bathroom."

Danny jumped out of the car. "There's Zachery playing with his wagon!" he said.

"Bring in some groceries, kids. You can take a minute and help," Marlene persisted as she opened the trunk and began unloading some of the bags. But Danny was already running off to Zachery's house and Jennifer was headed for the bathroom.

Marlene slammed the car door and yelled, "Danny, come back here!" Danny continued to run down the sidewalk toward Zachery. "They make me so mad. This isn't how it should be. Children are supposed to listen to their parents," she muttered as she felt her anger grow inside.

Trying to calm down, she brought in the groceries alone. "Why won't they obey?" she thought in frustration. "I wish they'd do what I tell them the first time. They just ignore me . . . Life sure would be easier if these kids would learn to think of someone other than themselves." Marlene decided that she would talk to their father, Craig, about it when she got a chance. The children must just be in a negative phase right now.

The next day, Danny went to nursery school. For the past two years he had been attending the Trinity Christian Preschool three mornings a week. He seemed to like it, often coming home singing songs and talking about fun things he did. Craig and Marlene appreciated the Christian influence and the way the teachers tried to apply the Bible to the children's daily activities. Marlene was able to work for a local doctor on those mornings. The extra money was helpful, and she liked the opportunity to be around other people.

When Marlene arrived to pick up Danny, she paused at the window to watch the class for a few minutes. The children seemed happy and content and

Mrs. Santos, the teacher, was calm and in control. Marlene wondered how she could care for these children, getting them all to cooperate, and still remain so cheerful.

When Mrs. Santos saw Marlene, she told Danny to put away the game he was playing with. Danny picked up the pieces, put them in the box and put the box back on the shelf.

Marlene was amazed. Danny had obeyed quickly—more quickly than he did at home. In fact, as Marlene observed Mrs. Santos give some more instructions to Danny and the other children, she was surprised to see that they were listening to her and obeying right away. "What's her secret?" Marlene thought.

Opening the door, Marlene entered the classroom and greeted Mrs. Santos. "I really appreciate the way you interact with these children," Marlene began. "I've noticed how Danny responds to you. Do the children always obey you when you tell them what to do?"

Mrs. Santos smiled. "Well, it didn't start out this way. It took a few weeks for the children to learn that I mean what I say. Now they know I only say things once and if they don't obey, there are immediate consequences. It took a lot of work those first few weeks but, as you can see, the children are happy when they understand our classroom rules and know that my action point is pretty tight."

"Action point . . . what's that?" asked Marlene, puzzled.

"An action point is the point when you stop talking and you start acting," Mrs. Santos explained. "Many parents are frustrated with their children for not obeying, but in essence they have taught their children that they don't have to obey quickly. A tight action point is the secret to prompt obedience."

"I'm not sure I understand," responded Marlene, a little confused.

"Let me ask you something. If you tell Danny to get ready for bed and he doesn't do it, what happens next?"

"Well," said Marlene after thinking a moment, "I tell him again."

"And what else?" prodded Mrs. Santos.

"I guess I usually raise my voice."

"Does he obey then?"

"Not usually. Most of the time I have to tell him three or four times before he obeys. It gets so tiring. It seems I have to get angry and yell at him before he takes me seriously."

"I think that by giving Danny several warnings you've taught him that he doesn't have to obey you the first time," observed Mrs. Santos. "I know you're trying to follow God's principles in raising your family. The Bible gives many helpful insights for family life. I like the verse in Matthew 5:37 which says, 'Let your "Yes" be yes, and your "No," no.' In this passage Jesus is teaching that extra words shouldn't be needed to validate our statements. We should mean what we say when we say it. I think this can be applied to parenting. Danny needs to know you mean what you say without you having to yell or repeat yourself."

"But I tell him that he should obey me the first time."

"Yes, parents often say that, but do you really mean it?"

"Of course I mean it."

"Then why do you give several warnings or ask several times? Why don't you discipline him right away?"

"I guess I never thought about it that way," Marlene replied. "Are you saying that, in essence, I've taught Danny that he doesn't have to listen to me right away?"

"Exactly," smiled Mrs. Santos. "A tight action point teaches children to obey our first instruction."

Marlene glanced at her watch and realized she needed to leave. "Mrs. Santos, you've given me something to think about. Thanks so much for sharing this action point idea with me."

"Well, having a tight action point doesn't solve all of the problems, but it does help quite a bit. I've learned a lot working here and raising my own children. If you want to talk some more, why don't you give me a call and we could set something up."

"Great! I'd really like that. Thanks again," Marlene said as she took Danny by the hand and headed out the door.

As Marlene drove home she thought about her action point. It seemed strange to her that the same

Danny who would wait until she said something three or four times would respond to Mrs. Santos the first time.

Later that afternoon, Marlene was busy in the kitchen. As she made dinner, her thoughts returned to Danny's teacher and what she had said about a tight action point.

Noticing that both children had left their coats in the kitchen, she called, "Jennifer and Danny, please come and get your coats and hang them up on the hooks." No response.

Marlene knew they heard her but they weren't moving. "I'll bet they'd move pretty quickly if Mrs. Santos were giving the instruction," she thought.

That got Marlene thinking about other adults who spent time with the children. Just yesterday, Craig was straightening up the house after dinner. "Danny, I need your help for a few minutes to pick up around here. I'd like you to clean up those blocks." Danny immediately left his puzzle and went over and cleaned up the blocks. "I'd like you to go out and get the ball and bat off the front lawn and put them in the garage." Again Danny responded quickly.

Later, when Craig asked Danny to clean up his puzzle because it was time to get ready for bed, Danny paused. Marlene remembered that Craig expected an immediate response and when he didn't get it, he began moving toward Danny who quickly decided to obey.

Last week, Danny's Uncle Patrick took the children to the park near their house. When it was time to leave, Marlene walked up to meet them. Patrick called to the children and, although reluctant, they responded and came running over. Marlene knew that if she had called them, there would have been a bout of complaining and arguing. Patrick had a great relationship with the children and they had a lot of fun together, but when Patrick gave an instruction, they obeyed. She realized that Patrick had a tight action point.

Karla, the babysitter, often had trouble with Danny. Marlene and Craig had Karla stay with the children each Wednesday night while they went to their church small group meeting. This past Wednesday Danny was acting wild before they left and Karla was unable to get him to settle down. She told him to stop jumping several times but he just ignored her instructions. She never did get to an action point. Craig had to step in and speak to Danny himself.

"I'm telling Mom!" Marlene's thoughts were interrupted. It was Jennifer's voice coming from the living room.

"You make me so mad!" Danny yelled.

Marlene turned off the stove and headed for the living room. Danny's words were echoing in her head. Those were her very own words. She used them when she was getting frustrated that her children were not obeying. "I don't believe it. Is that what I sound like?" Marlene thought.

After Marlene talked to Jennifer and Danny and helped them work out their problem, Jennifer went outside to play. Marlene returned to the kitchen, but Danny's words still penetrated her thoughts. *"You make me so mad."*

"I don't like the way that sounds. I've got to do something different before my children learn bad habits." As Marlene thought about her anger, she realized there was a connection between her anger and her action point. "I'd like to find a way to get them to respond to me before I get so angry. What would happen if I tightened my action point?" she wondered. She decided to try a little experiment.

Marlene went into the living room where Danny was playing with blocks on the floor. She said, "Danny, come hang up your coat."

Then Marlene went back into the kitchen and peeked around the corner. Danny was still playing with blocks as if nothing had happened. "Danny," she called politely, "if you don't come hang up your coat right now I'm going to send you to your room."

Danny continued to play. Marlene returned to the living room and said, "Danny, because you didn't obey, you need to go to your room."

Danny was shocked. He usually had more warning than this.

"But Mom!" he groaned.

"No, you didn't obey. You need to go to your room," Marlene said firmly.

Angry and confused, Danny stomped to his room. After several minutes passed and he had time to settle down, Marlene went to talk to him.

"Danny, why didn't you obey me the first time I told you to put away the blocks?"

"I don't know," Danny sulked.

"Because I tell you to do something over and over, you must think you don't have to obey me right away. We're going to change this. From now on I am only going to say things once. I want you to obey the first time. Do you understand?"

"Yes," Danny agreed.

"God has given me a responsibility as your mom to teach you how to obey," Marlene continued. "I'm trying to learn how to do the right things as a parent, and you are trying to learn how to do the right things as a child. We need to keep working together in order to be the kind of family God wants us to be."

Marlene realized the importance of her action point. She normally would have thought that the solution was to be more strict. Now she realized that, for her, "being strict" meant being harsh. Instead, she now wanted to tighten her action point. She knew that there were no easy solutions and that changes would take place over time. This action point idea was a great place to start.

Understanding the Secret

Secret #1 - The Secret to Prompt Obedience is a Tight Action Point.

How often have you told your son to get ready for bed, and then had to say it again and again before he started to move? . . . or have you told your daughter to pick up the toys and then found them still spread all over? How long does it take to get your teenager off the phone? or to mow the lawn? One of the solutions to these kinds of problems is a tight action point, but that means some changes in mom or dad first.

Sometimes parents get pretty attached to the ways they relate to their children, even when those ways are a part of the problem. Improving children's behavior sometimes requires change in the parents first. The secret shared in this chapter involves some changes in you before your children will change, but when you see the potential blessings, you'll be willing to make those changes.

By making small adjustments, you can bring about significant changes in your home. This first secret is foundational. If you apply it in your family, you will see immediate results. It will train your children to obey more quickly. It will bring immediate change in your child's behavior. It's something that you can put into practice today.

Children are unique. No one approach works all the time, but there are some truths of parenting that can be applied to all children. Action point is one of them. One way to see immediate improvement in children's behavior is to tighten your action point.

An action point is the point when you stop talking and you start acting, or the point when children know you mean business. You already have an action point and your children know what it is. How do they know? You give them cues. Sometimes you get out of the chair or you start moving toward the kitchen where that special utensil is. Maybe you raise the pitch or volume of your voice, or you use their middle name. You may start moving toward them or touch them.

The important thing about an action point is that children know when they must obey and they know that they don't have to obey until you get there. Each adult has a different action point. The rules are a little different in the classroom than they are on the playground, or in the home. That's why when Dad says it, the child may jump into action, but with Mom that same child may not respond as quickly. Babysitters may get taken advantage of because they often have very little action point.

There's a children's time bomb game which illustrates this idea of an action point. The time bomb is wound up and then passed around the group of children until it pops. That time bomb has an action point. In fact, after you play the game for a while you'll learn to anticipate when it is about to blow. Some children will hold it while it's ticking and then pass it just before it goes off. They know its action point.

Parents, you are like this game and your children learn how to play you. They continue what they're doing up until the point when they know you'll take action. Your children know your action point. They know when they need to obey.

There are four important things to remember about your action point.

Action Point

1. An action point teaches children when they must obey.

2. Action points vary among people who discipline.

3. Children learn to respond to each person's action point.

4. Being consistent with a tight action point is hard work, but it is worth it in the end.

For many parents, anger is the motivation for their action point. A raised voice is a typical indicator that action is imminent. Anger, however, can be a destructive emotion, causing more damage than good to the relationship. When you get angry with your children's lack of responsiveness to your instruction, you would do well to use that anger as a flag to remind yourself that your action point is not tight enough. You've allowed the situation to progress far beyond where it should be, and your anger has finally motivated you to take action. It would be better to back up a few steps and take action sooner in the process.

An action point determines the rules of the game for both parent and child in the discipline process. If you try to change your action point without explanation, your children may feel hurt and resentful. Although you have never clarified it before, you have taught your children to respond the way they do. If you're going to change the rules, it will be helpful to explain to your children what you're doing.

Sit down and have a talk with your child. Explain that you have been wrong in teaching them to respond slowly when God expects them to respond quickly. From now on you're going to ask them once, then comes the action. In this way they'll develop the character quality of obedience.

Practice is important. Give children many opportunities to obey as they're learning the new action point. Practice in places and at times when you can work through the process. In our seminars we're often asked "the grocery store question." It usually goes something like this: "What if my child acts up in the grocery store, what should I do?" Action point is a skill that needs to be practiced but it's best to practice in safe, easy places. The grocery store is like the final exam. If you practice enough at the park and at home, then children will respond properly in the public places too.

Children will occasionally test the action point to see if it's still there. Don't disappoint them. Firm boundaries provide security for children.

Offer much praise to the child who responds. As you work on the action point idea, remember that the tight action point works in a positive way as well. Immediate praise for work well done is very motivating. It's very important to catch children doing the right thing. Not only do you want to affirm behavior but you want to encourage the character development that you observe. Use words like, "You are becoming very obedient. I like the way you are learning to obey." Praise goes a long way to build good habits.

Tightening an action point requires that parents make important changes in themselves first. It takes work, but if parents tighten their action point then children obey more quickly. When parents realize that children need to learn obedience and that they, as parents, are the ones to teach it, then the individual acts of disobedience become very important opportunities. When you understand that teaching obedience is an important part of your role as a parent, you'll be more motivated to keep a tight action point.

But I Hate Conflict

Most people naturally try to avoid conflict . . . and why blame them? Conflict situations inevitably are inconvenient, irritating or downright painful. Furthermore, the continual correction needed with most children wears parents down, leaving them with little energy to persevere or be consistent.

Parents must realize, however, that obedience is a very important character quality to teach to their children. In fact, Ephesians 6:3 reminds us that children should learn to obey and honor their parents, so ". . . that it may go well with you and that you may enjoy long life on earth." Obedience brings life and freedom. When children learn to obey, *they* are the beneficiaries. Taking time to teach obedience is in your child's best interest.

When you understand the importance of obedience in your child's life, you'll be motivated to make some changes. Working on your action point is a great place to start!

The secret to prompt obedience is a tight action point.

Secret Two

The Secret To Constructive Discipline

"Jennifer, it's time to go. Did you make your bed?"

"No, Mom, I forgot."

"You forgot! You know you have to make your bed before you go to school. Now you're late. Get your lunch. I wish you wouldn't dawdle so in the morning!"

Jennifer rushed to gather her things.

"If you can't get everything done in the morning, you'll have to go to bed earlier," Marlene continued.

"That's not fair," Jennifer said, beginning to cry.

"You waste too much time in the morning," her mom argued. "It's too late now. Hurry, or you'll miss the bus!" she said as she rushed Jennifer out the door.

Jennifer ran to the bus stop, carrying her lunch and coat and wiping the tears from her eyes. Marlene watched her from the window and sighed, "Another frustrating morning . . ."

Yesterday didn't start any better. Marlene had just said good-bye to Jennifer at the front door when she heard a crash inside the house. She came running in and there was Danny, standing in the middle of the living room, and her new lamp was lying on the floor.

"What happened!" Marlene yelled.

"The ball hit the lamp," Danny replied quietly.

"Take that ball out of here right now and go find something to do!" Marlene scolded.

Danny picked up the ball and walked slowly out the door with his head down.

An awkwardness was left between them, the same tension Marlene felt now as she watched Jennifer run to catch the bus. She didn't like being so negative with the children but it seemed like every day was a battle.

"I wish I could do something about the tension around here," Marlene thought.

Later that day, Marlene had her neighbor, Bridget, over for coffee.

"I had a hard morning," Marlene complained.

"You did? What happened?"

"Jennifer just dawdles around in the morning and then isn't ready when it's time to go to school. Today she didn't make her bed. I wish she would pay attention to what she needs to get done."

"So what'd you do?"

"I was pretty hard on her. We both got angry."

"How'd you leave it?" asked Bridget.

"Not too well. She was crying when she left the house and I was still frustrated."

"That does sound like a hard morning."

"Maybe the real problem is that I don't like the way I left things with Jennifer. I really don't like being so negative, but I don't know what else I could have done," Marlene added sadly.

"I know what you mean. A couple days ago, Justin was playing in the yard and he dug with his truck in my flower bed and broke some of my flowers. I got angry and yelled at him. We both ended up feeling bad as he went off and played down the street. Later I realized I needed to do something with Justin that Bill and I have been working on with both of the children."

"Really, what's that?"

"When Bill and I discipline our children, we're trying to bring some kind of closure by having what we call a positive conclusion."

"What do you do to end positively?" asked Marlene.

"We usually ask three questions and give one statement."

"You mean you always do the same thing?" Marlene challenged.

"Well, not always, but we usually cover the same ground each time. I regretted not doing this with Justin the other day and so later I went and got him and we talked about it."

Marlene was curious. "What are the questions?"

"The first question is, *'What did you do wrong?'* We want to make sure they understand why they are being disciplined. When I asked Justin, 'What did you do wrong?' he answered, 'I played in the flower bed.' "

"Okay, then what do you ask?"

"The second question is *'Why is that wrong?'* When I asked Justin this, he said, 'Because you told me to stay away from the flower bed.'

"Then I said to him, 'You're right. You weren't obeying.' "

Bridget continued, "The third question is, *'What are you going to do differently next time?'* When I ask this, I want the child to think about a better way to handle the problem or frustration. Justin answered, 'I'm going to stay out of the flower bed.' "

"You make it sound so easy," smiled Marlene. "I'm not sure my children will answer these questions."

"I understand what you mean. I was surprised at how much Justin and Chrissy could figure out. The point is, we're trying to get them to learn from the discipline. We want it to be a constructive time."

"I think some kind of a conclusion like this would help me feel better about the problem," Marlene observed.

Bridget responded, "When I saw that Justin was sorry and willing to do the right thing, it was easy to forgive him. We both felt better."

"That sounds better than the way I left it with Jennifer this morning."

"The statement we end with is, '*Okay, go ahead and try again.*' This tells children we believe in them and we want them to keep trying. It's like saying, 'You made a mistake, but that's no reason to quit.' "

"All this sounds good," Marlene said, "but I'm not sure it would have worked this morning with Jennifer. I probably shouldn't have disciplined her when she was trying to get out the door."

"Maybe. It's hard to discipline when you're in a hurry."

"It might have been better to work a little ahead this morning or to save it for this afternoon when she got home from school," Marlene said and then thought for a minute. "Do you talk about the problem this way every time you discipline?"

"We usually do," affirmed Bridget. "That's why I felt bad when Justin went off to play. A positive conclusion is very important so we want to get it in there somewhere."

"This sounds interesting. Maybe I'll talk to Jennifer some more when she gets home."

"I think you'll find that helpful," said Bridget as she got up to go.

As Bridget said good-bye and walked back home, Marlene reflected on her interaction with Jennifer that morning. They had both been frustrated. Having a positive conclusion would have been nice.

"Jennifer, I'd like to talk to you," began Marlene when Jennifer got home. They sat down on their couch and Marlene continued, "I've been thinking about this morning. I want to tell you that I'm sorry for speaking harshly to you on your way out the door. That wasn't the best way to handle the problem. Will you please forgive me?"

"Okay," said Jennifer.

Marlene went on. "Let's talk about what happened. Do you know what you did wrong?"

Jennifer looked down and said, "I didn't make my bed."

"That's right," Marlene agreed. "Why was that wrong?"

"I don't know," said Jennifer.

"Well, you didn't get all your work done before school, did you?" Marlene prompted.

"No."

"Remember, we talked about what you need to do before school. We each have jobs we need to do in the morning," Marlene explained. "Do you understand?"

"Yes," answered Jennifer.

"What are you going to do differently next time?"

"I'll make my bed."

"That's good. Let's try to do better tomorrow, okay?"

"Okay," Jennifer said. "Can I go over and play at Cara's house now?"

"Yes, I think that would be fine. But first you need to make that bed."

"Okay, Mom," Jennifer said smiling.

"Can I give you a hug?" Marlene asked, realizing that something had happened in her daughter. She wasn't quite sure if it was her smile or the look in her eyes but the positive conclusion was helpful. As hard as it was to work this through, it seemed that Jennifer was feeling better. The process seemed to brighten her spirits. Jennifer gladly reached out and hugged her mom before she bounded up to her room.

Marlene felt better, too. The air seemed to be clear between them. She knew that this problem was something they'd continue to work on but for now, at least, the slate was clean and there was a freshness in their relationship.

"This is great," she thought. "Finally, I've worked through an issue with Jennifer and we both feel good afterwards. I really want to do this every time I discipline."

Understanding the Secret

Secret #2 - The Secret to Constructive Discipline is a Positive Conclusion.

Disciplining children can be like working on a craft project. I[*] have a needlework project that has been sitting in a bag in my closet for several years. I spent a lot of time picking out the right color thread, choosing the pattern and then working on the project, but it hasn't  been enjoyed by anyone. I made it to be displayed, but it's been packed away because I didn't complete the job. I won't gain the benefit of this project until it's framed and hung on the wall.

Discipline is like that. Sometimes parents feel that once the consequence has been given, their job is finished. They've done their duty and fulfilled their responsibility. Unfortunately, there may be tension left in the relationship and children feel guilty or may plan revenge. True repentance may not have taken place. This leaves room for anger or even bitterness to linger. Discipline is not complete until the relationship between the parent and child is restored. The child needs to understand the wrongdoing, but also feel the unconditional love and acceptance from the parent.

---

*Joanne

Parental anger often creates tension between the parent and the child. The parent further punishes by putting distance in the relationship. This is unnecessary and unhelpful. The secret to constructive discipline is a positive conclusion. The real benefit comes when discipline is framed, finished off and completed with a positive conclusion.

The positive conclusion can mean the difference between punishment and discipline. Punishment focuses on past misdeeds; discipline focuses on future good deeds. Punishment looks for justice in order to balance the scales; discipline teaches a correct response and helps the child learn wisdom. Punishment is negative; discipline is positive. Punishment is motivated out of anger; discipline is motivated out of love. The positive conclusion turns what otherwise might be punishment into a constructive learning experience.

A positive conclusion is a discussion you have with your child. Use it every time you need to correct or redirect your child. Talk about the problem and what went wrong; then talk about what could happen differently next time. One way to have a positive conclusion is to use the process Bridget has suggested to Marlene.

During the early stages of development (ages two to eight), the structure of three questions and a statement gives children a helpful pattern each time they're disciplined. Although two- and three-year-olds may not initially be able to respond appropriately, it's helpful to begin this pattern when they're young. You may need to walk preschoolers through the process in order for them to benefit from it. Four- to eight-year-olds will quickly learn to expect these questions and a statement and be able to learn from the experience. As children grow older, you may want to put aside the structure and look more to the principles behind it.

At any age it is helpful to spend some time discussing the problem in order to end the discipline time on a positive note. The positive conclusion isn't a time of interrogation. It's important to express love, forgiveness and acceptance during this discussion. A closer look at these three questions and a statement will show the benefit each one offers in making discipline times constructive learning experiences.

The first question is, "What did you do wrong?" Ask it in a tender way, not accusing. This allows the child to admit personal sin. It's important for the child to take responsibility for part of the problem and demonstrate sorrow for it. If others were involved, as they often are, a child should not excuse an offense by blaming someone else. The sins of others don't justify wrong actions. It's probably not uncommon for two children to come to you arguing and fighting, blaming the other child for the problem. "He hit me." "He grabbed my book." Almost always, both children are wrong and could have responded differently. It takes two selfish children to have a fight.

A common mistake here is that parents often engage in dialog about the whole situation: who else was wrong and whether it was fair or not or why such things happen. Those discussions may be helpful, but you'll get much further if you start by asking "What did *you* do wrong?" and allow the child to take responsibility for his or her own part of the problem.

Sometimes children say they don't know what they did wrong. If they truly don't know, it's okay to prompt them. If, on the other hand, they are trying to avoid responsibility, it's often helpful to give them time alone until they are ready to own their part of the problem.

Parents discipline their children in a variety of ways and for different issues or problems they see. Disobedience, character weaknesses and childish irresponsibility provide opportunities for you to teach your children. The positive conclusion facilitates the teaching process and the first question helps children take responsibility for their actions and admit fault.

A second question, "Why was that wrong?" should be used to address heart issues directly. Point out the character qualities like pride, selfishness, anger, or disrespect. Help the child learn that behavior is only a symptom of something deeper. Parents and children see the behavior but God looks on the heart. If Sally grabbed the book, Karen still needs to learn to respond with kindness and self-control.

Most children, at first, have a hard time understanding why their actions were wrong. The positive conclusion gives you an opportunity to gently teach, without preaching. Help your child see that a particular response was unkind or disrespectful. Discipline involves teaching.

The "Why?" question and its answers provide opportunities for parents to teach children about the ramifications of wrong choices. The book of Proverbs teaches that parents are a source of insight and discernment. Naivete and immaturity lead one to do foolish things. Actions are foolish when they have unforeseen bad results. Parents can use discipline times to teach children to anticipate the consequences of their actions.

Once a child realizes why the behavior is wrong, the third question helps clarify what should be done instead. "What are you going to do differently next time?" focuses on a better way to respond. The wise parent uses this question to continue teaching. By communicating the right response verbally, your child will begin to see the difference and learn to change. This often takes time and repeated discipline sessions.

Questions such as the ones we've mentioned here can help the parent teach a repentant child significant truths about Godly character.

Finally, always end with an affirmation. A helpful statement is, "Okay, go ahead and try again." This says "I believe in you. Yes, you're going to make mistakes, and there are consequences, but we can debrief and learn together." Give children the encouragement to try again. Everyone makes mistakes, and the best response is to stop, think about it, and then try again.

A positive conclusion is important every time you discipline. It is the secret to making your discipline times constructive experiences. The Bible tells of a number of occasions when Jesus affirmed the people He disciplined. In John 21, after He rose from the dead, Jesus spent time with Peter to reaffirm their relationship. In the same way that Peter had denied Christ three times, Jesus gave Peter the opportunity to reaffirm his love three times. After each affirmation, Jesus responded to Peter with a command to do ministry. Jesus commissioned Peter and told him to go and do the right thing. In essence, Jesus said, "Peter, you made a mistake. I still love you. Go and serve me." Imagine the guilt and embarrassment Peter had lived with for several days. He knew that he had disappointed his Lord and his conviction caused bitter weeping. Jesus cleared the air and gave Peter the newness of relationship he needed.

A woman was caught in adultery and became a victim of the harsh and judgmental religious leaders of the day. Just imagine how she must have looked, sad, dejected and wilting as they brought her to Jesus. The Pharisees had their own problems which Jesus addressed first, but his gentle handling of the woman is instructive for us. He said to the woman the same kind of thing we want to communicate to our children, "Go and sin no more." He wasn't justifying her sin but He was giving her a fresh start. His final words to her were an affirmation of her as a person and an encouragement that she was competent and capable to do the right thing. That's the kind of ending to discipline that children need.

The positive conclusion is an essential part of the discipline process. Going through the three questions and a statement provides a framework which allows children to admit that they were wrong and determine what to do right next time. The positive conclusion gives an opportunity for you to communicate your trust and faith in your children as you tell them to go out and try again.

After the positive conclusion, the child may need to complete restitution or reconciliation, enabling the child to establish a clear conscience. Unresolved conflict hinders a clear conscience. A child needs to have the opportunity to say, "I was wrong, please forgive me," and then feel forgiven. The child may need to pick up the books that were thrown in anger or comfort a sibling he offended and then feel the relationship restored.

When discipline times are ended with a positive conclusion, the air is cleared and relationships are renewed. Everyone feels better. The distance or tension is gone because conflict is resolved. Children shouldn't have to go around bearing the weight of unresolved conflict or the disappointment of their parents.

The positive conclusion is essential for effective discipline. Parents are not to simply administer consequences. They must teach their children a better way to respond. A conclusion like this gives the opportunity to make sure everyone understands what was wrong and how to do better next time.

A Positive Conclusion

1. *It's a discussion at the end of the discipline when the problem and consequence are clarified, teaching takes place and relationships are restored.*

2. *It makes the discipline process a learning experience rather than just a negative punishment.*

3. *It might consist of three questions and one statement:*
   What did you do wrong?
   Why was that wrong?
   What are you going to do differently next time?
   Okay, go ahead and try again.

4. *It helps the child know what to do right next time.*

5. *It reestablishes the relationship, and encourages the child to try again.*

6. *It prepares the way for restitution and reconciliation to take place and enables the child to establish a clear conscience.*

Secret ♡ Three

The Secret To ♡ Helping Children Choose To Do What's Right

"Danny, it's time for your bath."

"I don't want to take a bath."

"Danny, I told you that you were going to have to take a bath this afternoon. Today is Sunday. We won't have time tomorrow."

"But I don't want to take a bath. Can't I do it later?" Danny whined.

"No, Danny, you need to take one now. Go into the bathroom."

Danny stomped into the bathroom pouting, obviously angry about having to take a bath.

"Danny, stop. We need to talk about this. Your response right now isn't good."

Danny turned around and looked at the floor in front of his mom.

Marlene continued, "Your response needs to be 'Okay Mom' and then go and do it."

"Okay Mom," Danny said with a sigh. He got into the bathtub, but it was clear to Marlene that something wasn't right. She had been noticing that

Danny had a pattern of doing what she asked while continuing to hold onto a bad attitude at the same time. As Danny played in the bathtub, Marlene stopped by the den where her husband was working on the computer.

"Craig, I think we've got a problem."

"Another one?" he smiled.

"I don't think our discipline is effective enough."

"What do you mean?"

"Well, sometimes when I discipline the kids, their behavior changes but I can tell that their attitude is still a problem. They seem to be obeying on the outside just so they can get on to what they want to do next."

"Marlene, I need to finish up this letter. Why don't we talk about it some more tonight after Jennifer and Danny go to bed."

"Okay," Marlene said as she left. Maybe talking about it tonight will help.

Craig realized that his wife was discouraged. He knew she was right, though. The children did seem to have some attitude problems and even though they obeyed, those negative attitudes lingered on.

That evening after Jennifer and Danny were in bed, Craig and Marlene sat down on the couch with some tea.

"It reminds me of what Pastor Dave was saying this morning about the importance of repentance and changing the heart," Craig said as he and Marlene began their discussion. "Remember in his sermon he was talking about how God looks on the heart."

Marlene thought for a moment. "Yes, but he was talking about church discipline. They excommunicated the person who was sinning in order to motivate that person to repent. Kicking our kids out of the family seems a little extreme, don't you think?" she asked jokingly.

Craig laughed, "I'm not suggesting that, but I do agree they need to repent and change their heart, not just their behavior."

"How do you think we get them to change their hearts?"

"I don't know. There seems to be a big difference between church discipline and family discipline. I wonder what Pastor Dave would say," Craig continued.

"Why don't we call him and find out?" Marlene suggested.

"Okay, that's a good idea. I'll call him now." Craig looked up the number and dialed the phone.

"Hello, Pastor Dave? This is Craig. Marlene and I were just talking about your sermon this morning. Do you have a few minutes to talk about it?"

"Sure," Pastor Dave replied. "What would you like to talk about?"

"We've noticed that our children often obey but still have a bad attitude. You talked about changing the heart this morning. Do you have any suggestions about how to help *children* change their hearts?"

"That's a great question, Craig. Annie and I are trying to work on that with our children too. We want to help our children understand that God looks at the heart. That's a very important part of our discipline with them."

"How do you do that in your family?" Craig pursued.

"When our children have a problem, we have them take a Break. They need to sit down somewhere alone to think about the problem and their attitude.

"Today, when we came home from church," Pastor Dave continued, "Joe threw his coat on the floor. When Annie asked him to pick it up, he responded with grumbling. Annie had him hang up his coat and then told him to take a Break until he could come and talk to her with a good attitude."

"Then what happened?" Craig questioned.

"A few minutes later, he returned and talked with Annie about his bad attitude. Joe admitted that he was wrong and it was obvious that his attitude had improved."

"Take a Break? That's interesting. Don't you feel bad sending children away when they've done something wrong? I don't want to communicate that I don't love my kids or don't accept them."

"I understand what you're saying, and I believe this must be done in a very loving and gentle way. We're not sending a child away in anger; we're just giving the child an opportunity to stop and think about the problem. In a sense, we gave Joe a Break to settle down and organize his thoughts a little so he could respond more appropriately."

"So you don't see this so much as a punishment, just a chance to settle down?" Craig clarified.

"Yes, that's right. We want children to understand why their behavior was wrong. We want them to *want* to do the right thing for the right reasons."

"That seems like a lot to expect from a child," observed Craig.

"It takes time to develop this kind of approach with children. I'm convinced that only God can change the heart, but we can do a lot to prepare the child for God's work. Young children often just need to settle down and come back to the parent who will help them process these things. Older children, with practice, can often think through much of the process themselves."

"I like this idea," affirmed Craig. "I'm not sure how to get started, though. Danny's only four."

"It sounds like you're on the right track," said Pastor Dave encouragingly. "Discipline can be pretty complicated. Sometimes a Break can give children just what they need. Then they're ready to come back to the parent and receive some teaching that's necessary. Taking a Break can help to prepare the heart for further guidance."

"Okay, Pastor Dave, I really appreciate your insights. Marlene and I are going to talk about this some more. Thanks a lot."

Craig hung up the phone and shared with Marlene the things Pastor Dave had said. They decided they would look for ways to help Danny and Jennifer change their attitudes, not just their behavior.

"Focusing on the heart seems like a pretty important secret to parenting," Marlene concluded.

"Let's try this," Craig agreed. "Next time one of the children has a bad attitude, let's have that child sit alone for a few minutes, then, after settling down, come back and talk about the problem."

The next morning Marlene saw her chance to try out this new secret. She had asked Danny to pick up his pajamas off the floor and hang them on his hook.

"Not now, Mom," protested Danny as he headed downstairs.

"Danny, come back here. I want you to do it now, before you go down to breakfast."

Danny turned around and huffed back to his room. Marlene watched from the door as Danny hung his pajamas on the hook.

"Danny, I want you to come talk to me," she said calmly.

Danny walked angrily over to his mom.

"The attitude I see shows me that you are obeying on the outside but your heart is not right. I want you to go and sit on the stairs and think about your heart. Come and see me when you're ready to talk about this with a good attitude."

Danny trudged over to the stairs and plopped himself down. Marlene went down to the kitchen to make breakfast.

At one point Danny started getting off the stairs to pick up his car at the bottom landing.

"No, Danny, you need to sit still and quiet until you're ready to talk to me," Marlene reminded.

After about ten minutes, Marlene saw Danny come into the kitchen and stand quietly.

"Are you ready to talk about it?" Marlene asked. She could tell that Danny was trying to do the right thing.

"Yes," he said calmly.

"Danny, do you understand what the problem was earlier?"

"I didn't want to hang up my pajamas."

"That's right, and your response showed a bad attitude. It's important to do the right thing *and* have a good attitude. I want to help you learn this. Do you understand?"

"Yes."

Marlene gave Danny a hug and he went bounding over to the table to eat his breakfast.

"Well, that went pretty well," thought Marlene. "I really like to see him respond with a good attitude. I'm going to concentrate on the heart more instead of just focusing on behavior with the children."

Understanding the Secret

Secret #3 - The Secret to Helping Children Choose to Do What's Right is to Focus on the Heart.

Craig and Marlene were right in seeing the importance of addressing more than just behavior. The Scriptures emphasize that God's primary interest is the heart.

When Samuel was looking for the first king of Israel, he wanted to choose Eliab, one of Jesse's finest-looking boys. God informed Samuel that, "Man looks at the outward appearance, but the LORD looks at the heart."

The wise parent looks beyond behavior to what's going on at a deeper level. This involves the child's attitudes and motivations. The goal of all discipline is not only to help children act correctly and think correctly, but also to be the person that God wants them to be. God doesn't just want us to do the right things. He wants us to be the right person.

Many parents work hard to help their children look good on the outside by concentrating on behavior. Inadvertently, these parents teach their children "image management," the ability to appear good, clean and nice on the outside. When those same children reveal unresolved issues of the heart as they grow older, their parents are devastated. "What is happening? My child was so obedient for years, now this?" they wonder. Some of these same parents recognize too late that their parenting style dealt efficiently with behavior change but left the heart virtually untouched.

Some children find it easy to connect their actions with heart issues, but most children tend to separate the two. Billy, a preschooler, was told to sit down. He said, "No." The teacher, not wanting to be outdone, leaned over Billy and said sternly, "You sit down!" Billy sat down and replied, "I'm sitting on the outside but I'm standing on the inside." Too many children are like Billy, changing their behavior in response to discipline but continuing to disobey in their hearts. They may be harboring resentment, selfishness or anger.

The Scriptures contain a valuable principle, which, when applied, enables parents to address the heart. The principle of separation provides the opportunity and the motivation for children to make heart-level changes.

As you begin to use the secret of teaching children to focus on their hearts, you will see them make attitude adjustments, not just behavior changes. You will find yourself getting to the root of disobedience or immaturity and helping children make lifelong changes. Most importantly, right before your eyes, you will see your children begin to choose the right course of action.

Taking a Break

All parents realize the futility of trying to teach an unrepentant child or a child caught up in emotions. A Break can motivate right thinking and prepare the child for teaching. This technique can allow the child to settle down in order to benefit from the discipline time. Of course, parents who have been in the habit of shaming their children, or punishing them, will find that this discipline may take a little getting used to.

A Break removes a child from a situation or activity immediately following misbehavior. A reminder of the rule may be helpful and the child is instructed to take a Break to change the heart. The location for the Break is a place away from any activity or stimulation. The child shouldn't talk to anyone until ready to return to the parent. The parent also shouldn't dialog with the child until the child is ready to come back. Other benefits of family life are suspended while the child is working on the heart. A Break allows the child, under the guidance of the parent, to determine when to come back and talk about the problem. When used correctly, a Break can help children look deeper than behavior and see the need to allow God to work on their hearts.

A Break is not the same as time out. Many Christians have a hard time with time out, and for good reasons. Typically, time out is a term used for isolating a child as a punishment for doing wrong by simply sending that child away for a set period of time. This is "punishment by isolation" and can be counterproductive to the discipline process. Expecting children to solve problems alone is unrealistic. Furthermore, the isolation can appear to force children away from the love of the parent.

A Break is a much more valuable technique because, if done correctly, it focuses on the heart.

We're not suggesting that parents should always use a Break in place of spanking or other consequences. In fact, it may be used in conjunction with other methods of discipline. We are saying that just administering a consequence and walking away isn't enough. That often doesn't address the heart. Some children are able to put the two together, but most of the time children need help processing heart issues. Just ask yourself how many times have you corrected your child, spanking or other discipline, and come away feeling like you've not accomplished your goal? Something isn't working. Your child is simply not changing.

A Break is different. Instead of punishment by isolation, the Scriptures teach discipline by separation. There are two models which use this principle of separation to motivate repentance. The models are examples of ways that the Biblical principle of separation is applied to bring about repentance.

The Principle of Separation in Scripture

To understand the Biblical basis for taking a Break, it is important to look at the principle of separation in Scripture. Exploring two models is helpful, our Heavenly Father's relationship to His children and the relationship of the church to the unrepentant sinner. A Break draws three distinct characteristics from these models: the goal is repentance, the motivation to change is a feeling of missing out on family involvement, and the child helps determine the length of time spent in the Break.

The goal of a Break is repentance. The first model, the relationship of our Heavenly Father to His children, illustrates the principle of separation. When we enter God's family, we have forgiveness through Christ, but when we sin, we are separated from fellowship with Him.

A Break teaches children a more accurate picture of reality. There is a loving God who hates sin. When His children disobey Him, they experience separation as a natural consequence of disobedience. God lovingly waits for them to return to Him with confession and repentance.

God never separates Himself from us physically because He is spirit, but a spiritual separation between us and our Heavenly Father develops. Christians experience this separation through guilt and a lack of peace, and then become motivated to repent and regain intimate fellowship with God. Separation from fellowship with God motivates the believer to repentance.

<u>A Break provides the motivation to repent by allowing the child to experience the feeling of missing out on involvement in family life.</u> Parents can force a child to change actions but they can't force a change of heart. Parents can, however, motivate children to change. The second Biblical model, the relationship of the church to the unrepentant sinner, further applies the principle of separation as a motivation to change. Passages about church discipline in the New Testament reveal two factors which motivate sinners to repent. In 1 Corinthians 5:2 Paul expresses grief or sorrow over sin. When parents reflect sadness instead of anger, they provide an effective motivation for a heart change to take place in their children. The disappointment seen in a parent's eyes can be a powerful motivation for a child to want to change.

In the New Testament, when a believer was unresponsive to correction, the consequence was separation from the benefits of the church fellowship. In Matthew 18, Jesus established a pattern for discipline within the church which had as its final consequence separation or excommunication. In 1 Corinthians 5, Paul encourages the church to put the unrepentant man out of the body. This separation would cause the offender to miss the benefits of the fellowship and would motivate repentance.

In the model of the relationship of the church to the unrepentant sinner, the principle of separation is used as a last resort. In the family, the principle of separation is applied a little differently. Because separation can motivate repentance, a Break can be helpful as part of the discipline process rather then being viewed simply as a consequence.

Through the principle of separation, children learn that a person cannot enjoy the benefits of the family without also abiding by the principles which make it work. Parents, while communicating unconditional love, teach their children that separation is the natural consequence of disobedience.

<u>The child helps determine the length of time spent in the Break.</u> Since repentance is the goal, it's hard for a parent to tell when a child is ready to return. To come back from a Break too soon may short-circuit what God wants to do. To remain too long may cause unnecessary discouragement. The model of the relationship of the church to the unrepentant sinner addresses this problem. In 2 Corinthians 2:7 Paul encourages the believers to welcome back the repentant person and not to continue the separation past its intent. He says, "You ought to forgive and comfort him, so that he will not be overwhelmed by excessive sorrow." Some children take longer to change their hearts than others. The wise parent will be able to discern from the child's face, posture, and tone of voice whether repentance has taken place, or at least that the emotions have settled down so the child can move on in the discipline process.

The best solution is to allow the child to help decide when it's time to come back. This is a primary difference between the Godly model of a Break and that which is often practiced in time out. The length of time a child chooses to stay in the Break isn't important except as it relates to the child's needs. Frequently all that's needed is a reminder and the child is ready to change the heart and try again. In this case, the Break would be short, taking only a few seconds. Other times, because of stubbornness, a change of heart may take longer, twenty minutes or several hours. Either way, the child is encouraged to initiate when the Break is over.

	Time Out	A Break
Goal	punishment	repentance
Focus	behavior	heart
Length of Time	determined by parent	determined by child
Role in Discipline	a consequence	part of the training process
Responsible Party	parent has responsibility for the child's reentry	child has responsibility for making changes and returning
Attitude of the Parent	emphasizes distance between parent and child	emphasizes the parent's desire for the child to return

How Do Children Change Their Hearts?

A complete change of heart takes a lifetime, but God's work of grace motivates small, day-to-day changes to accomplish this greater work. Small steps of right thinking and attitude adjustments contribute to lifelong patterns of godliness. It would be unreasonable to expect a lazy child to instantly change to a diligent one. So what *do* we expect from a child when taking a Break?

One day, I[*] asked my sons, "What happens in your heart when you take a Break? I see that when

---

[*]Joanne

you start the Break, you're angry and when you come back you're changed."

Timothy (age five at the time) responded, "I think about it and I'm sad I did it."

David (age seven at the time) said, "I think about what I did wrong and I feel sorry."

Children may not understand how it happens but with practice they are able to make heart level changes. Repentance, in children, involves several steps:

1. Stop fighting, calm down, and be willing
   to talk about the problem.
2. Acknowledge wrongdoing.
3. Be willing to change.
4. Commit to doing right.

These are all steps that a child can do. Ideally we would also like to see two other steps of repentance take place:

5. Feel sorry for wrongdoing.
6. Have a desire to do what's right.

These last two steps of repentance, however, often involve a work of God's grace in a child's heart. You can't force a child to completely change the heart. Only God can do a thorough transformation of inner desires and motivations. There are a number of things that a child can do to set the stage for God's work to take place. Children can change their thinking, values and attitudes. They can calm down and acknowledge wrongdoing. Parents and children can then pray that God will give them a complete change of heart.

Sometimes children may only settle down (Step #1) while they are separated, then they can come back and process the other steps with the parent. Other times, children will develop such a sensitivity to God that He can make significant heart changes. When the child returns in those times, you will see a difference in the heart as it is reflected in the child's face, posture and attitude.

The only prerequisite for coming out of the Break is that the child be willing to work through the repentance process. The child may be ready to change, but not know what right behavior to implement next time. Remember, repentance is a condition of the heart. Once the child has begun a change in the heart, then the parent can help the child learn what was wrong and what is a more appropriate response.

Children who are young or are just learning how to take a Break may find it difficult to identify what they did wrong, why it was wrong, or even know how to think about the separation. Other children aren't even ready to think because they're too caught up in their own emotions. In situations like these, the purpose of a Break is simply to change the heart by settling it down in order to return for a teaching time with the parent.

One of the key factors leading to change in a child's heart is the Holy Spirit. Working through a child's conscience, the Holy Spirit makes significant inroads into the child's attitudes and motivations. A Break slows down the discipline process and gives God the opportunity to work on deeper issues in the child's life by challenging the child to look past behavior to the heart.

Using a Break in Your Family

From a very practical standpoint, a Break can be an excellent way to deal with much of the day-to-day correction children need. It can become the primary discipline technique used in a family to help children change. The three-year-old who screams out of frustration, the seven-year-old who continually interrupts, and the thirteen-year-old who teases relentlessly all need to understand why their actions are wrong and see the need to change the heart as well as their habits of behavior.

At first, children may resist a Break. Some may not want to lengthen the discipline process; they'll try to get it over with too quickly. These children are especially in danger of modifying behavior without repentance. It's important for children to learn how to take a Break and make sure their heart is responding properly before they move to the solution.

Children may try to come out before they are ready or they may defiantly move out of the place where they were told to sit. The parent's responsibility is to teach children that they must obey. A parent may restrain them by holding them in place or firmly putting them in the correct spot again. These actions are best accomplished with as few words as possible so as not to encourage the rebellion by giving attention to it. The parent must win in these situations in order to make the Break an effective discipline in the future.

Even children as young as three or four years old, although not able to understand the word "repentance," can understand having a soft heart or removing rebellion from the heart. Older children are able to process some of what went wrong and come back to the parent with a specific plan for what to do right next time.

Sometimes children, especially those who are just learning to take a Break, want to come back before they are ready, or they choose to stay there longer than necessary. The parent then must help them to process their emotions and learn to initiate the conclusion of the discipline appropriately.

One day when my[*] daughter Megan was seven years old, she was yelling at her brother. I called her upstairs to talk to me about it and she began yelling at me. I sent her to take a Break for a bit and settle down. About a minute later she came back but was obviously not changed. Her head was tilted down, her posture was slumping and her bottom lip was sticking out. I didn't even have to talk with her. I just told her what I saw. "Megan, I can see that you're not ready yet. The way you're standing and the expression on your face all tell me that you still have a

[*]Scott

problem in your heart. I want you to continue your Break until you're ready to come out with a changed attitude."

This time she stayed away for about twenty minutes and when she returned she was obviously different. In fact, I took her head in my hands and looked deep into her eyes and said, "I can see your heart in there. It looks pretty nice right now. It looks like you're ready to talk about this." Megan giggled and we continued to talk about the problem in a way that she could understand and respond to.

A Positive Conclusion Follows the Break

It is helpful to follow a similar process each time the child comes back from a Break, talking about the problem to help the child process what happened.

When the child first comes back, ask, "What did you do wrong?" This allows the child to admit personal sin. It's important for the child to take responsibility for part of the problem and demonstrate sorrow for it.

A second question, "Why was that wrong," addresses heart issues directly. Point out the character qualities of pride, selfishness, anger, or disrespect. Help the child learn that behavior is only a symptom of something deeper. Parents and children see the behavior but God looks on the heart.

The third question, "What are you going to do differently next time?" helps children understand and communicate what right action should take place next. Talk about positive character qualities to develop. Identify ways to show honesty or kindness or humility.

Questions such as these and their answers can help the parent teach a repentant child significant truths about Godly character. Be sure to end the positive conclusion with an affirmation. Encourage the child to "Go ahead and try again."

Children who are upset may have a bad attitude when they take a Break. Habitual bad attitudes must be confronted. When they come back from the break, first deal with the offense that needed discipline, then have them take another Break because of the bad attitude. You may say something like "I'm disappointed that you had a bad attitude when I told you to take a Break. Since you didn't have a good attitude, I want you to take another Break. When you are ready to talk about your attitude, then come back and see me." When the child returns, talk about the attitude.

A Break may be just the beginning. When a child has begun to change the heart and has discussed the problem, a consequence is sometimes still necessary. A parent may say, "Tommy, I'm glad you understand why pushing and hitting are wrong. Because you were having a difficult time playing with your brother, you need to play by yourself for awhile." A Break prepares a child to receive correction, understand the consequences of behavior and be willing to change.

A Break is just one discipline method. Children must realize that parents have a number of resources. Spanking, losing privileges, natural and logical consequences, and child/parent evaluation meetings are just a few methods parents can use to mold children's behavior. Each has benefits and when used in combination, provide maximum growth opportunities for children. In most families, it's not effective for parents to rely solely on one form of discipline. A parent may say, "It looks like you're not responding to a Break. If a Break doesn't work, I have something else that will." It is beneficial for parents to have a toolbox of discipline techniques.

When you use a Break with your children, they will learn how to think rightly about their hearts and what motivations prompt their behavior. With practice, it will give your children a mature approach to dealing with their hearts.

How to Use a Break

1. *Quickly begin the Break after misbehavior is evident (within 5 seconds).*

2. *Stay calm, remain businesslike and matter-of-fact.*

3. *State the offense. For example, "No whining."*

4. *State the directive, "I'd like you to take a Break," or "I think you need a Break."*

5. *The Break location may be any place which is separate from the place of activity. Break spots vary depending on the situation and the age of the child. A younger child may sit near a wall in the same room or in the hall. Older children may go to their rooms.*

6. *Ignore protests, pleading, excuses, even tantrums or questions.*

7. *If a young child refuses to take a Break, pick him up and gently put him there and say, "You need to obey." As a parent, you must win.*

8. *Don't talk to a child who is taking a Break except to clarify the Break instructions.*

9. *Allow the child to come out of the Break when he/she has at least calmed down, and is ready to talk about the problem.*

Secret STOP Four

The Secret To
Raising Wise Children

"Jennifer won't stop squirting me!" complained Danny as he ran into the kitchen.

Craig put down his pen and went to the back door for the third time that morning. "Jennifer! Stop squirting your brother!" he yelled.

"Danny, you go back out and play," Craig said, turning and walking back to his chair.

Fifteen minutes later Jennifer was calling, "Dad, Danny keeps shaking my table and I'm trying to color." Now they were in the playroom. Craig looked up from his bookkeeping and called, "Danny, stop shaking the table!"

"I'll never get these bills paid this way," he grumbled, opening the next envelope.

As the bickering continued in the other room, Craig began to think, "Why do they tease each other so much? I feel like I'm constantly telling someone to stop." Craig leaned back in his chair. "I wish they'd have more respect for each other and show a little kindness. I've got to do something about this."

"I want you two to come here," Craig called from the kitchen. Jennifer and Danny came and stood by their dad. "I'm trying to get some work done while your mother is out, but every few minutes I have to stop and solve your problems. I want you to stop annoying each other and get along."

"But Danny won't stop bothering me," Jennifer complained.

"If Danny is bothering you, I want you to tell him to stop. You don't need to call me."

"He doesn't listen to me," she persisted.

Craig turned to his son. "Danny, if Jennifer asks you to stop, I want you to stop. Do you understand?"

"What if she's bothering *me*?"

"Then you can tell *her* to stop, and she needs to listen to you. Okay Jennifer?

"I want you to learn to respect each other and to listen to each other's words. Are you ready to try?"

Both children nodded.

"Okay, let me finish up here. You both go play." Craig picked up his pen and continued working.

When Marlene arrived home twenty minutes later, Craig was taking the bills out to the mailbox. "I think we need to do something about this bickering between Jennifer and Danny," he suggested to his wife.

"Did you have a hard time this morning?" Marlene asked as they walked into the house.

"They were bickering and irritating each other and they kept coming to me and tattling."

"That sounds familiar," agreed Marlene, with a little sarcasm in her voice.

"Well, after stepping in a few times, I got frustrated. I don't want them being so unkind to each other. I feel like a referee around here."

"I feel that way sometimes, too," Marlene sighed.

"I talked to them about it this morning."

"What happened?"

"I told them that they need to listen to each other. If they don't like something the other one is doing to them, they can say 'Stop' and the other one has to listen. I think we should make this a rule for our family."

"Okay, we could try that. How did it work this morning?" Marlene asked, a little skeptical.

"Well, it's too soon to tell, but I like the idea of having them try to work things out together before they come tattling."

"Do you think they'll listen to each other?"

"That's the whole point. I want them to *learn* to listen to each other," Craig explained.

"Don't you think you're asking too much? They're still young."

"Yes, I know, but if we could teach them to respect each other's words, we'd be teaching them something important. At some point they've got to learn to work things out and listen to each other. This kind of rule will give them some wisdom about life and teach them something they can use forever."

"I agree with you there. Let's just see what . . . "

Suddenly Jennifer burst into the kitchen. "Dad, I told Danny to stop and he won't stop!"

"Here we go," thought Marlene.

"Danny, come here!" Craig said firmly. "Jennifer, you stay here too. Let's talk about this. What happened?"

"We were playing with the dominoes," Jennifer began. "We were standing them up in a line and knocking them down. Then I wanted to play by myself, but Danny kept knocking mine down. I told him to stop, but he kept doing it!"

"Is that right, Danny?"

"I was just playing," Danny defended.

"But you didn't stop when your sister said, 'Stop,' right?"

"Yes."

"Okay, this is the new rule we talked about this morning. I want you to learn to listen to someone else when they say 'Stop.' Danny, you need to play by yourself in your room for awhile."

Frustrated, Danny turned and headed for the stairs and Jennifer went back to the playroom.

Marlene looked at Craig and smiled. "Maybe this will work," she said encouragingly. "I really like the idea of having rules that teach them to respect each other."

"One thing still bothers me though," Craig said thoughtfully.

"What's that?"

"Well, the 'Stop' rule, if we can call it that, is

okay for teasing and annoying, but what about when they start to argue with each other? What kind of rule can we have to teach kindness and respect when they are having a problem like fighting over a toy?"

"That's a good question! It's those kinds of problems that make me feel like a referee!" Marlene said with a laugh. "I never know who had it first or who started the problem. Whatever I decide, somebody complains, 'That's not fair!' "

A few hours later the whole family went out into the yard to rake leaves.

"I want the red rake!" Danny called, running to the shed.

Jennifer was there first and quickly grabbed the red rake.

Danny stopped and turned to his mother whining, "Mom! Tell Jennifer to give me the rake."

"Jennifer . . ." Marlene began.

Craig interrupted, raising his hand, "Wait a minute, Marlene. *We* don't need to choose who gets the red rake."

Marlene paused, waiting for Craig to continue.

"What's the problem, Danny?" Craig began as he tried to think of a better way that his son could approach the problem.

"She always gets the red rake," Danny complained as he walked closer to his dad.

"I want you to go talk to Jennifer about this instead of complaining to your mom."

"But she won't give it to me," he argued.

"Danny, I've got a plan," began Craig as he bent down closer to his son. Then, almost in a whisper, he continued, "You go over to Jennifer with a good attitude and say, 'You had the red rake last time. Could I have it today?' Maybe she'll let you use it."

Danny smiled and ran to the shed. Marlene and Craig stood watching and listening, wondering if their children really could negotiate.

"You had the red rake last time. Could I have it today?" Danny repeated.

Jennifer looked at Danny and then at her parents watching from halfway across the yard. "How about we take turns," she offered. "I'll use it first and then you can have it."

"I want it first," Danny persisted.

"Okay, you can have it for a little while and then it's my turn."

"Okay," Danny agreed. Jennifer handed him the rake.

Craig and Marlene looked at each other, smiling in surprise. Marlene nodded and said, "This is great! They came up with a better solution than I would have."

"Yes," affirmed Craig, "if we develop some rules for communication like this, they may learn about negotiating and communicating with each other more effectively. I'm sure it won't happen like this all the time but it's something we can work toward."

Understanding the Secret

Secret #4 - The Secret to Raising Wise Children is to Use Family Rules to Teach Values.

Craig and Marlene established some rules to teach their children how to respect each other in the midst of conflict. These rules teach principles that will benefit Jennifer and Danny for years to come.

Rules are an extension of values and principles. They are the practical application of what one believes. Rules are values put into action. They show children what values look like, how to put them into practice and why they are valuable. If you want your children to embrace the values you hold dear, you need to teach them what they are and how to implement them in their lives.

The Turanskys have rules about manners at mealtime. We have seven people eating around the table, so if someone wants something on the other side of the table, we've taught our children to say three things: the person's name, "would you please pass," and then the item they would like. "Give me the butter" is not acceptable because it is not showing thoughtfulness to others at the table. "Melissa, would you please pass the butter," is the acceptable way to ask. Furthermore, it seems that some children think that "amen" is the Greek work for "go," so when the prayer is over they begin the meal in a rather selfish way. In our family, when we're done praying, instead of asking for others to pass something, we encourage the children to look in front of them for what needs to be passed and offer it to the next person.

One family was teaching this to their children. Five-year-old Jack took the plate of chicken and offered it to his three-year-old sister, Cheryl. "Which piece of chicken would you like?" he asked.

Being a young girl and not knowing much about the anatomy of a chicken, she said, "I'll take the hand."

Jack, a little frustrated, but hanging in there, replied, "Cheryl, a chicken doesn't have a hand. Pick something else."

Cheryl, relishing this attention, but still not quite understanding, said, "Okay, I'll take a foot."

Jack was getting hungrier by the minute and his patience was wearing thin. Mom and Dad were trying to control themselves so as not to burst out laughing. Jack said, "Cheryl, chickens don't have hands or feet. They fly. Pick something else."

Cheryl, wanting to be cooperative, thought through the list of body parts she knew and said, "Okay, I'll take the head." To which Jack replied angrily, "Mom doesn't cook the head."

Cheryl, knowing she better do something quickly, said, "Okay, just give me the belly button."

Mom and Dad couldn't handle it any more. They were roaring with laughter as Jack put the platter

The Secret to Raising Wise Children

down, grabbed a piece of chicken and said, "Here, take a breast. That's about as close to the belly button as I can get."

Manners are a good way to teach children the value of thoughtfulness.

Some parents, when they find their children misbehaving, just create more rules. Rules don't solve the problem though. Children can learn to obey and mind the rules but their hearts may remain untouched. Values address the heart. "Please share your bike helmet with your sister." That's obedience. "Are you being loving?" addresses a value. Teaching values will equip children to be versatile, having the ability to adapt to new situations.

This is especially important when working with teens. When children become teenagers they begin to create their own value system. If parents only spend time creating rules, then they're expecting their young people to translate those rules into everyday life and make their own determination about what's really important. This is often unreasonable for the teen. Teaching values prepares children of all ages to apply the rules in different ways to new situations.

Can you remember any rules you had as a child? Were you expected to obey without knowing why? Sometimes parents enforce rules for which they, themselves, don't understand the significance. Maybe you were expected to keep your room neat and tidy. Did you know that this rule was intended to encourage cleanliness, organization or self-discipline? One of the best ways to teach values is to talk about them in connection with family rules. Unfortunately, if rules are separated from their underlying values or principles, then the rules may be viewed as prison bars and tossed aside at the first opportunity. When this happens and a rule is abandoned, then the underlying value may be completely missed. When establishing and enforcing rules in your family, talk about the values they represent.

If you're just starting your family, it is most helpful to simplify the rules as much as possible. You may want to start small with three basic rules. These rules are actually values and become the basis for most other rules within the family. Almost any infraction in family life comes under one of the following rules:

- Obey
- Show Respect
- Be Kind

Talking about these three basic rules will lay the foundation for your children to develop values.

The Value of Responsiveness to Authority

Two essential values taught during the preschool years are self-discipline and responsiveness to authority. A number of rules can be used to teach these values to your children.

First, children must learn to come when they are called. You're not going to get very far in the discipline process if you call your son and he runs the other way. Parents who don't teach their children to come when they are called can be seen yelling across the parking lot or down the block. If a four-year-old child is two houses away and you want to talk with him just call his name, "Brian!" Teach him that when he hears you call his name he needs to come. He shouldn't yell, "What do you want?" If he does, only say his name and ask him to come, "Brian, come here please." Don't carry on a conversation by yelling. As you teach Brian to come when he's called, he learns responsiveness to authority. When Brian does come, he needs to be within a few feet and say "What Mom?" or "What Dad?" This is one of the very first rules you can teach.

Now you may be thinking, "That's fine for you, but my kids won't come." Getting to the point where your child comes when you call will probably take some practice. I[*] am going to tell you how I taught this to Timothy when he was young. First, I had to explain to him what I expected. I said that from now on, whenever I call you, you need to come close to me and say "What Mom?" I explained that it was important that he learn to listen carefully to my words and when he heard me call, he needed to come to me and find out what I wanted. I explained that since I was his mother, he needed to learn to listen to me. Then I tried it out.

Timothy was about two and a half years old. The most natural thing for a child to do when you call is to yell back, "What do you want?" I had to refrain from answering the question and just repeat my request, "Timmy, come here." When Timothy finally did come, I reviewed with him the new rule.

I practiced this rule every chance I could. I didn't only want to call him when I needed to discipline him or when he was running away from me in the store. I practiced at home and at the park. I called him often just for fun. "Timmy, come here." When he came I'd say things like "I just want to tell you I love you!" or "I just want to see how well you can obey."

Timothy liked the game. He'd beam from ear to ear when we played it and I praised him for coming quickly. Sometimes he would initiate the game himself. He'd say to me, "Mommy, call me and see how fast I come." It started as a game for him, but children learn through play. Timothy learned to respond to my authority and developed a sense of accomplishment at the same time.

The "Come When You're Called" rule is one way to teach responsiveness to authority. It can be taught to children at a young age as they begin to learn foundational values.

The Value of Self-Discipline

In addition to responsiveness to authority, young children need to learn self-discipline. The following is a story of how we[*] taught our youngest children the value of self-discipline.

---

[*]Scott and Carrie

When our adopted girls, Elizabeth and Megan, first came to us, they were not very self-disciplined. They were four years old but would often run away from us in public places. They were energetic and eager to touch things and explore their world. We would go into someone's home and they would disappear and come back with a prized stuffed animal off someone's bed or a decorative piece off of a shelf. It was embarrassing. We knew we needed to do something quick. We started with the "No Touch" rule.

I chose to teach this rule at a time that was convenient for me. I explained to the three young children (our natural son, Ben, was also four at the time) that when we entered someone's house or a store, they were not allowed to touch anything without first getting permission. I then announced that I was going to the auto parts store and invited all the children to go with me. Three four-year-olds were eager to go. I reminded them about the "No Touch" rule and told them that children who can obey the "No Touch" rule could go to the store with me. I spent about fifteen minutes in that store, mainly supervising my children. I told them that I would come over and look at things that they saw. I would pay attention to them but they couldn't touch anything. We almost got out of there with a successful experience but then Ben brought me something. "Dad, look at this."

"Oh, Ben," I said sadly. "I'm so disappointed you picked that up. Go put it back."

I paid for my merchandise and when we got out of the store we debriefed about the "No Touch" rule. I told Ben that if he couldn't obey the "No Touch" rule I wouldn't be able to take him on special trips to the store.

About a half hour later, as is often the case when you're trying to fix something on your car, I had to return to the auto parts store. I announced that I was going, and as four-year-olds typically do, they all wanted to go again. (It's funny that young children get such joy out of simple trips to the store. When they get older you've got to think of much more complicated things to delight them.)

I said, "Oh, Ben, I'm sorry. I'm not going to be able to take you with me this time because you touched something last time. I want you to stay home and think about that."

Crying, Ben stayed home with Carrie. The girls jumped in the car and off we went. We talked about the "No Touch" rule on the way there and on the way home. It was a successful experience. A little while later I made yet a third trip in which we took Ben again with us and he had a successful time also.

I didn't tell them that we were developing self-discipline but that's what it was. After about six months of practicing that rule in the video store and the grocery store, in the bank with those aisle markers and in neighbors' houses, the children had learned the rule. They had developed enough self-discipline that I could take them into a gift shop and they wouldn't touch anything. In fact, we soon began receiving compliments for how well-behaved our children were. Occasionally they would make a mistake and we would quickly have them sit down right in the store and think about the "No Touch" rule.

All was going well until the Saturday I went to a repair store to get my lawn mower fixed. I remember that day well. My three younger children weren't touching a thing but they were jumping around, playing tag and just being rambunctious in the store while I was talking to the salesman. Someone said, "Whose kids are these?" I felt like crawling into a hole. That's when I developed another self-discipline rule, the "Don't Be Wild" rule.

We use this rule when we go into public places, libraries, stores, museums and church. It simply means that we are careful to control ourselves in certain public places so that we are honoring to others. The "No Touch" rule and the "Don't Be Wild" rule are examples of ways that we taught our children the value of self-discipline at a young age.

The Value of Your Words

As Craig and Marlene discovered, the 'Stop' rule is another rule for family life which teaches an important value and should be observed by parents and children alike. When any child wants to be done playing a teasing or tickling game, he or she can say 'Stop' and the other person must stop immediately.

Establishing a 'Stop' rule allows children to set limits on others' behavior toward them. It allows any child, young or old, to set a boundary and to know when that boundary is violated. This levels the playing field among siblings so that all family members can feel safe and know that they can use their words to protect themselves.

Setting up boundaries such as these in the home helps children learn to set limits in other areas of their lives, too. When children are in the habit of recognizing boundaries, defending them, and getting help, they are less likely to become silent victims of abuse.

Since children are sometimes selfish, they can misuse this boundary idea. That is, they ask for the game to stop temporarily so that they can get the upper hand and then restart the game. A child being tickled may say 'Stop' only to turn around and tease back. This can add an element of confusion to the 'Stop' rule and should not be allowed. Rather, words like "Times" or "I'm on base" are better for temporary pauses in a game. The 'Stop' rule should be used for ending the game.

Boundaries such as the 'Stop' rule are not useful unless there is a place to appeal. When children believe their boundaries are being violated they must have somewhere to turn. It's important for parents to be available to help children use the 'Stop' rule appropriately and to respond to each other's words.

The Value of Thoroughness

The preteen and teen years seem to be the age when parents become taxicab drivers, shuttling children to friends' homes, sports events, music lessons, and church activities. Most parents don't mind shuttling children back and forth because of the benefits of those activities for their children. But occasionally parents get surprised because after they have given permission for their child to go to an activity, they find that they are also the chaperone or are responsible for picking up other children or going to get them at some late hour of the night. Parents don't usually mind sacrificing in these ways for their children. It's the surprises that catch parents off guard which sometimes create frustrating experiences. Children can be taught to bring a 'complete proposal' to parents when asking permission for activities. Here are several questions that could be included in a 'complete proposal.'

What do you want to do?
Where will it take place?
Who's in charge?
Who's driving?
When do you need to be there?
When and how will you return home?
How much will it cost?
How will you accomplish your other responsibilities while you are gone?

By thinking through the answers to each of these questions, children learn to take many factors into account when making a decision. These questions help a child to think through how their request affects others as well as how it affects themselves and their own responsibilities. The 'complete proposal' teaches children to think carefully about all that's involved in a particular choice they want to make. By giving each other as much information as possible, parents and children both know what to expect. Differing expectations are one of the leading causes of conflict. Developing the value of thoroughness in decision making can prevent some of the anger that might otherwise occur.

Melissa came to me[*] one day and asked if she could watch a special movie. As she progressed through the 'complete proposal' I found out that she was asking me to go to the video store to get the movie and that she had not yet finished her laundry. Once we had all the facts, we were able to work out a plan and she was able to watch the movie that evening.

Understanding the value behind the family rules you establish and enforce allows you to teach your children important truths in very practical ways. Parents can teach in other ways, such as modeling, illustrating or lecturing, but giving specific guidelines in the form of rules helps children learn success principles on a day-to-day basis. Craig and Marlene realized they could teach their children about kind-

---

[*]Scott

ness and respect by setting up rules for handling disagreements.

As authors, we could fill this book with practical ways to teach values to children, but you can do the same thing. What kind of rules do you have in your family? What do they teach? Why do you teach your children not to interrupt someone when they're talking? Why ask permission before borrowing someone else's toy? Why do children clear their plate from the table when they're done eating? Why should children put toys away after they're finished playing with them? Behind each one of these rules is a value children can embrace.

Furthermore, parents can create new rules to teach values they sense are lacking in their family. For example, if your children are being mean to each other, then you may teach some new rules that emphasize the value of kindness. Besides all the don'ts—don't hit, kick, yell, grab or push—positive demonstrations of kindness can be expressed. "You must take others' feeling into account as you make choices and play games." "Except for rare situations, you should share a toy you are not using." "Include all those who want to play." These and other rules help children understand how to be kind in practical ways. Rules are an excellent teaching tool for communicating values to children.

How to Make Rules into Lessons Which Teach Values

Sometimes parents have the rule first and then search for the value, but it's most helpful to work from values to rules.

1. *Determine the problem that needs to be addressed. Clarify it as specifically as possible.*

2. *Identify the value that is lacking. Define it in ways a child can understand.*

3. *Determine a family rule which puts feet to the value.*

4. *Proceed through the above steps with the child, when possible, to teach the value, not just the rule.*

5. *Remember that rules change as children grow older but the values and principles remain the same. More values and principles are added during maturity to balance and fill out the ones learned earlier.*

Many of the principles that apply in family life come from the Scriptures. It's good to show children ways that the Bible applies to their everyday life. Many good ideas exist in the world, but recognizing the Biblical basis for ideas makes them all the more powerful. The ideas for solving conflict expressed by Craig and Marlene actually come from Matthew 18 where believers are told that a person who has been offended should first go to the offender and try to work it out. If the offender refuses to listen then the Bible instructs the person to get someone else involved. This process, designed by God, provides children with a healthy conflict management plan, one they can use at three and four years of age as well as when they are adults.

Some time ago we[*] sensed a problem in our home with a lack of honesty. We had a rule, of course, about telling the truth, but Carrie felt like it needed to be backed up a little. The problem was that things were happening and no one was confessing to doing them, or when confronted there was some lying going on. Some of these things were hard to prove, so instead of trying to pin children down, she decided to deal with it in a positive way. Carrie's plan had a significant effect on our family life.

We spent a couple of weeks talking about what she called, "Honesty Under Pressure." She talked about the importance of honesty and read us stories like "The Emperor's New Clothes" and "The Boy who

Cried Wolf." She asked us each to tell about a time we chose to tell the truth under pressure, when it made us embarrassed or got us into trouble or we had to then apologize. Carrie developed an "Honesty Under Pressure" award which mysteriously appeared on children's doors who told the truth in difficult situations. The emphasis on a value made the rule come alive for us and significantly addressed a problem we were facing in our family.

Getting children to obey is part of parenting, but by no means is it the end. Teaching children values will help them to develop wisdom about life. You can teach values in a number of different ways, but one of the secrets to raising wise children is to use family rules to teach those values.

In this chapter we have given you some specific, practical ways to teach your children the values you want them to embrace. As you take time to establish and explain the rules you have in your family, your children will have the opportunity to learn principles which they will use for years to come.

It's good to remember that young children often have a hard time understanding abstract ideas like patience or kindness. As you establish rules to teach these concepts, you are giving your children concrete actions which they can put into practice. Rules put feet and hands on the values you want your children to learn.

As your children mature they will be able to understand the concepts behind the rules and embrace more fully the principles you are teaching. Older children will need fewer specific rules as they learn the intent behind them. They will make decisions and function based on the principles and values they have learned. Children will grow in wisdom and understanding as you teach them values through rules.

Secret Five

The Secret To Keeping Relationships Open

"Do your children always respond that way?" Craig asked after Brad finished disciplining his ten-year-old son, Aaron.

"What do you mean?" asked Brad.

"Your children are so responsive when you discipline them," Craig observed. "How do you get them to accept your correction without getting upset or angry?"

Craig and Marlene and their children were camping for the weekend with some of the other families from church. Brad and Annette Wilson and their four children had a campsite near to them. Craig and Marlene noticed that the Wilson children were responding to their parents' discipline without arguing or being defensive. There seemed to be an openness in their relationship that didn't shut down or close off when the children were corrected. Craig and Marlene were curious.

"Well, that's something we've been working on with them for years," Brad offered.

"Jennifer and Danny just aren't that sensitive. They don't seem to care that they're doing the wrong thing. They get angry when I discipline them," Craig reflected.

"I do think that children have their own personalities and some are more sensitive than others, but we've had to work hard at encouraging sensitivity and openness in our children."

"That's what it is," Craig observed. "I sense an openness in their relationship with you even during discipline times."

"I think it's because we don't discipline in anger," Brad said. "We try to respond to them with sorrow instead."

"Respond with sorrow? That's interesting. I'd like to hear more about this. Do you think Marlene and I could get together with you and Annette this afternoon sometime and talk?" Craig asked.

"Sure, our children will be going fishing in about an hour with Ralph and Joey. We could get together then."

"That sounds good."

While Jennifer and Danny continued to play at their campsite, Craig and Marlene went over to visit with the Wilsons. Pulling chairs up together, Craig began the conversation, "You make it sound like you choose sorrow over anger. I find that my anger comes on without a choice."

"Emotions are tricky—sometimes we're not even aware of what's going on," Brad observed. "I used to get angry and then, after the fact, wonder what happened. Now, even when I'm angry, I'm more tuned in."

"But anger isn't always wrong," Marlene objected. "Even Jesus got angry. When Jennifer or Danny disobey or are mean to each other, that makes me mad."

"Yes, anger comes pretty naturally to all of us," Annette agreed. "But anger is dangerous to relationships. It tends to put distance between people and make them defensive."

"That's a good point," Craig affirmed. "So what did you do to get rid of anger in your family?"

Brad laughed, "Well, I wouldn't exactly say we've gotten rid of it, but we've developed a plan to deal with it."

"What kind of plan?" Marlene asked.

Brad continued, "Several years ago we realized that anger was affecting our family. It was driving us apart and building walls between us. We decided we needed to do something about it. We began talking with our children about their anger and we all agreed to work on it."

"When our children were young, we started by helping them to recognize when they were getting angry," Annette added.

"Anger's pretty easy to see, isn't it?" Marlene asked.

"We wanted to recognize some cues before the children actually exploded in anger. We realized that each child gives warning signs that anger is coming. Those cues often go unnoticed until it's too late. We watched each of our children and helped them identify the cues that anger was approaching."

"So you could get ready for it?" Craig laughed.

Brad smiled. "Well, actually, we realized they needed to stop and recognize the cues so they could deal with the feeling before it got too intense."

"It seems like it would be hard to help children deal with *their* anger when I'm having trouble controlling *mine*," Craig admitted.

"I can sure relate to that," Brad agreed. "It's a humbling thing to teach children about anger. Then they recognize *my* sin more clearly. Working on this as a family has been quite a challenge, but we've all learned to apologize, forgive and love each other more."

"You said that you respond with sorrow instead of anger. I'd like to hear more about that," Craig suggested.

"We've just found that sorrow opens relationships while anger builds walls," Brad continued. "When we respond with anger our children become defensive. Sorrow is different. When we reflect sadness, dialog is opened and often children are motivated to change."

The conversation continued until the Wilson children returned from fishing. Craig and Marlene knew they were learning another secret, something that would bring significant change to their family life. As they walked back to their own campsite, Craig was already developing a plan. It wasn't long before he had the chance to test it out.

"It's my flashlight!" came Jennifer's voice from inside the tent.

"I just wanted to hold it. You don't have to grab!" returned Danny.

Craig walked calmly into the tent to see Jennifer and Danny arguing over the flashlight. Craig quietly said, "Danny, I want you to go out of the tent and leave the flashlight here."

"But I was just looking at it . . ."

"Go on, Danny. Obey me and go out of the tent."

"Jennifer," Craig began, "it makes me sad when you don't share with your brother. That doesn't seem to be very loving." Craig was watching to see Jennifer's response to his sorrow instead of anger.

"Yeah . . . but he'll just break it," Jennifer replied.

"Danny doesn't have a flashlight," Craig said softly. "I wish you would take time and allow him to use it instead of just demanding that he return it."

Jennifer didn't respond. Craig didn't know what else to say so he walked out of the tent. Jennifer had developed some pretty tough patterns of defensiveness. Craig wasn't sure his new response was working. She certainly didn't change her attitude on the spot.

Craig decided to build a fire for dinner and began to gather some wood. It hadn't been more than ten minutes since he had left the tent when he heard

Jennifer and Danny inside again.

"You can use it as long as you're careful," Jennifer said.

"Okay, I'll be careful," Danny replied.

Craig peeked in and saw that Jennifer was sharing her flashlight. "It worked," he thought. "That's nice, Jennifer," Craig affirmed. "I like the way you're being loving."

This was just a small step, but sorrow had worked better than anger. Craig realized that if he had allowed himself to become angry and had demanded that Jennifer share the flashlight, then they would all have ended up feeling upset and their relationships would be strained. By responding to Jennifer with gentleness and sorrow, he had encouraged a more compassionate side in her. Craig was determined to work on this more. This was a secret which would help to keep his relationship with his children open. Craig was excited.

Understanding the Secret

Secret #5 - The Secret to Keeping Relationships Open is to Have a Plan for Anger.

Anger is like the mercury in a thermometer. When left unchecked the intensity of the emotion increases from frustration to anger and then to other things like rage and bitterness. As the intensity builds, people shut themselves off from others and relationships close down. Having a plan to deal with anger can limit the intensity and prevent much of the destruction. A plan for anger can help keep the mercury from progressing up the thermometer and keep relationships open and healthy.

A plan to deal with anger will help you and your children develop healthy patterns. In this chapter you'll learn how to teach your children to recognize where they are on that thermometer at any particular time. You will learn how to equip your children with mature responses. By helping your children deal with their anger, you too may gain insights that will become part of your own personal anger management plan.

Most families don't have a plan for anger. They somehow just continue on, hoping things will get better. Many families don't resolve their anger, but just keep trying to start over. Starting over may be helpful at times, but it tends to ignore the problem rather than address it.

One day a man arrived home from work at his usual hour of 5:00 p.m. He discovered that it had not been one of his wife's better days. The result was that she had a short fuse and an unpleasant attitude. Nothing he said or did was right. By 7:00 p.m. things had not changed, so he suggested that he go outside, pretend that he had just gotten home and start all over again. His wife agreed.

He went outside, came back in, and announced in a loving voice, "Honey, I'm home!"

"And just where have you been?" she replied sharply. "It's 7 o'clock!"

Dealing with anger requires more than just starting over. You need a plan for addressing anger in your family.

Anger Can Be Dangerous

Anger is like a warning light on a dashboard. It flashes to say something is wrong. Sometimes, though, the problem is different than you'd expect. It has more to do with something going on inside *you* rather than an external cause. Some people develop such a problem with anger that the warning light stays on most of the time. It's set to go on at a low setting. It's helpful to understand your anger well enough to know how much of the irritation is caused by something around you and how much of your anger comes from something inside.

As you instruct your children about anger management, it's important to teach two general truths. First, anger isn't always bad, but it's always dangerous. When you're angry, you're likely to hurt someone. As children see the effect their anger has on others, they begin to see the need to control themselves.

The second truth children need to learn is that anger can be controlled. The way they respond to their anger is their choice. If a parent tells Susie to go to bed and she gets angry, the way she responds to the anger is up to her. Susie can stomp off and slam the door or choose to take a break and settle down. Children need to take responsibility for their actions, even when they're responding out of their emotions. They can't blame their bad responses on someone else.

Parents shouldn't blame their anger on other people either. Sometimes parents say, "You're making me angry . . ." in an attempt to motivate their child to obey. It's as if they're saying that someone else's behavior gives them the right to unleash their anger. Parents and children both need to learn to control their anger and choose to respond in appropriate ways.

An Anger Management Plan

Anger can be divided into four categories: frustration, anger, rage and bitterness. These words describe what people experience as the irritation they feel continues and is not dealt with properly. To effectively address anger they need a plan to deal with it in all four of these areas. Effective parents teach their children frustration management, anger control, rage reduction and releasing bitterness.

If you can develop a plan for anger and put it into practice in your home, you'll have closer relationships, be able to deal with conflict in healthy ways, and have a more peaceful family life. The following three-step plan will equip your children to recognize and process their anger in a healthy way.

Step #1: Identify the Cues

Children often don't recognize anger. In fact, many times they act out before they realize what happened. This first step helps children become more aware of their feelings and then more able to control them.

How can you tell when you're getting frustrated? How can your children identify frustration before it gets out of control? How is rage recognized? What are the indications that your child is becoming bitter or resentful?

Here are common cues in children that indicate they are experiencing some kind of anger:

- They tense up and clench their teeth.
- Their behavior or speech increases in intensity.
- They feel like crying or begin to cry.
- They say words that are unpleasant and their tone changes to whining or yelling.

- They become restless or withdrawn, unresponsive or easily provoked.
- They begin to talk incessantly.
- They make noises with their mouth like growls or deep breathing.
- They resort to violence, kicking, hitting, biting, grabbing, slamming, or stomping.
- They pout.
- They begin saying mean things or speaking disrespectfully.
- They engage in destructive activities, such as tearing a book or ripping a picture.
- They squint or roll their eyes or develop other facial expressions.

Take a few minutes and jot down the cues that each of your children show as they are getting angry. Parents need to first identify these cues for children and then teach them to identify the cues for themselves. Parents can point out that this feeling is called anger and that it needs to be handled in a specific way so that it doesn't get out of control. The job of the parent is to be a bridge for children, helping them recognize their frustration or anger and identify specific actions to take. When parents see frustration developing, they may help the child by saying, "I see you're getting frustrated. What are you going to do?"

If your preschool son is frustrated because he can't get his sneaker on, he needs to recognize that frustration before he gets so angry that he throws the sneaker across the room.

If your teenage daughter is frustrated because the blouse she wants to wear is in the laundry, or is wrinkled, you can help her recognize that frustration and know how to deal with it before it intensifies into anger or rage.

Eventually children will be able to see their own frustration and anger and choose appropriate responses. They'll be able to move from the emotion to the right actions. When parents step into the process to guide and train their children in anger management, their children learn to handle anger in positive ways.

Step #2: Step Back

One of the healthiest responses to anger at any of its stages is to step back. During that time the child can rethink the situation, calm down and determine what to do next. Frustrations can easily build, rage can be destructive, and bitterness is always damaging to the one who is angry. Stepping back can help the child stop the progression and determine to respond differently.

Sometimes stepping back means engaging in another activity or leaving the situation temporarily. Sometimes it means just pausing for a moment and taking a deep breath. A step back becomes a time to acknowledge that anger is developing and decide what course of action to take next. When you teach your children to step back and evaluate the situation, you are teaching them wisdom and maturity.

Step #3: Choose a Better Response

While children are stepping back they can decide on a more appropriate response to the situation. But what should they do? Parents who address anger in their children often respond negatively, pointing out the wrong without suggesting alternatives.

At each anger stage the child has several good alternatives which will lessen or remove the anger. When children are frustrated, they have three positive choices: talk about it, get help, or slow down and persevere. Simplifying the choices makes the decision process easier. Even young children can learn to respond to frustration when they know there are three choices.

If six-year-old Carl doesn't like the way Jack is playing with his favorite sports car, he should recognize the frustration and then decide to talk about it by saying, "I don't like it when you play rough with my car." Talking about the problem can help solve it without saying or doing something hurtful.

A second choice Carl has is to get help from another child or from a parent or teacher. A third party can give counsel and advice and help resolve the situation without anger.

Sometimes when children are frustrated, they can choose a third option: to take a deep breath and determine to persevere. Just acknowledging the frustration may allow Carl to continue to play with Joey without becoming angry.

Parents can help children learn to handle their anger by reflecting what they see and offering assistance without telling them what to do. Sometimes though, parents get caught up in their children's emotions and try to solve the problem for them. It's better to help children process their emotions rather than solve the problem. You may say, "You look frustrated. Remember, you have three choices." You may even offer help by saying, "If you need help, just ask me."

Sometimes children are too upset to continue. The anger they feel is so intense that they need to make some heart-level changes before they can respond with constructive behavior. Behavioral changes are only helpful and healthy when a child's heart is ready to release the anger. Forgiveness and sorrow are heart-level responses which can ease anger, rage and bitterness.

Forgiveness is much more than forgetting an offense. Forgiveness acknowledges the offense and chooses to let go of the desire for revenge, recognizing that God is the judge (Romans 12:18-19). Forgiveness means letting go and moving on, not holding the offense against someone any longer. Forgiveness is a mature and healthy response which says, "You have done wrong to me and much of that is between you and God. I am primarily responsible for my own actions and my response to you."

Sorrow is another helpful heart response which can reduce anger. Parents can model sorrow instead of anger when confronting their children. Craig responded to Jennifer with sorrow when she was unwilling to share her flashlight. Sorrow is a much more "relationship friendly" response than anger.

Young people would be more successful at changing the minds of their parents too if they would respond with sorrow instead of anger. The child who says, "I'm sad that I can't go over to my friend's house" is more likely to open communication about that subject than the child who is demanding and angry. Choosing to respond with sorrow invites communication and opens relationships.

Tantrums Are Not Just for Two-Year-Olds

Sometimes children progress beyond just anger. They become enraged. The primary way to tell when children are enraged is that they can no longer think rationally and their anger is now controlling them. They've lost control. You may see clenched fists, squinting eyes or a host of venting behaviors. Anger is one of those emotions that can grab you before you know what happened. The intensity can build from frustration to anger to rage before anyone realizes it.

When a young child is enraged, the parent calls it a tantrum. Children of any age can become enraged, though. Even some adults have a problem with rage; they just don't call it a tantrum anymore. Tantrums happen when anger is controlling the person. In general, tantrums are inappropriate responses to emotions and take on a variety of forms. They may be revealed through hitting, kicking and screaming, or they may involve hurtful words or withdrawal.

Whatever form it takes, rage needs to be controlled, not vented. Proverbs 29:11 says, "A fool gives full vent to his anger, but a wise man keeps himself under control." Allowing a child to vent anger is dangerous for the child and for anyone else around. If young children are taught to hit a pillow or a punching bag when they're angry, they won't learn to automatically stop that behavior when they get older and stronger.

One boy was taught to kick the furniture when he got angry. His mom called it "letting off steam." When he grew up he still kicked the furniture, his kids, his wife, his dog and anything else that got in his way. Venting anger teaches children an unhealthy response pattern. Anger control and rage reduction need to be taught to children early in life so they have the opportunity to develop habits of self-control and healthy communication.

Bitterness: The Ugliest Anger of All

Some people don't think of themselves as angry because they don't experience rage. Their frustration and anger go straight to bitterness. Anger has many faces and bitterness is one of the ugliest. Bitterness is much easier to deal with in children than in adults, but it is very dangerous nonetheless.

Bitterness is anger connected to hurt from the past, the ability to catalog painful memories so they can be used at any time to fuel present anger. Some indications that children are experiencing bitterness include:

- They may use words like, "You always!" or "You never!"
- They respond in anger more frequently and intensely than the situation warrants.
- They use sarcasm or become cynical.
- They become negative and critical.
- They withdraw and become unresponsive.

These symptoms don't always mean a child is bitter, but they may be indications of a problem.

The solution to bitterness is forgiveness. Don't ignore bitterness and resentment. Address it. Talk about it. It may mean listening to your children and communicating understanding. Resentful children sometimes feel like they are misunderstood and not listened to. You might say, "It sounds like you're still angry about not being able to go to your friend's house yesterday."

Parents tend to want to run from anger. They are afraid of it both in themselves and in their children. Some parents are afraid that they are going to deal with it the wrong way and so they don't deal with it at all. Bitter or resentful children need to see what their anger is doing to themselves. They are holding on to the offenses as a type of revenge. People were not created to carry around revenge. They have to let it go.

The solution for the resentful child is forgiveness. It's important that the parent continue to work with the child to resolve bitterness. Don't assume they're going to grow out of it. Rather, if it isn't dealt with, they'll grow into it!

Anger Prevention

There are a number of ways to prevent some of the anger children experience. These are long-term solutions and, when implemented, provide a well-rounded anger management program.

The first anger prevention strategy is to help children develop positive character qualities in order to alleviate some of the frustration and anger they now experience. Qualities like patience and tolerance look for ways to turn obstacles into opportunities instead of frustrations. Patience is waiting for something with a sense of contentment. Tolerance is putting up with an irritation without allowing it to provoke frustration or anger.

Some of the anger problems in children come because their character isn't developed to the point where they are able to manage their intense feelings. Teaching children to be kind, compassionate, humble, gentle, patient or forgiving, all help control anger. As children develop Godly character, they will experience fewer problems with emotions out of control.

Parents can also help reduce frustration and anger in their children by filling their emotional tanks.

Frustration is emotionally draining. Furthermore, when tanks are running low, frustration is less tolerable and the progression to anger and rage is accelerated. Children need to be hugged, touched, and verbally encouraged on a consistent and frequent basis. They need individual loving attention from their parents each day. Talk, listen, and make eye contact with them. Let them know they are valuable and important to you. Children with full emotional tanks can tolerate much more frustration than children whose tanks are running low.

Another way to prevent some of the anger in children is to identify ways that you as parents are contributing to an anger problem. Parents can exasperate or embitter their children (Ephesians 6:4, Colossians 3:21). Parental mistakes don't justify children's anger, but if there are some changes you need to make, it's best to acknowledge them and make the appropriate adjustments.

Sometimes frustrated parents become harsh and provoke anger in their children. Proverbs 15:1 says, "A gentle answer turns away wrath, but a harsh word stirs up anger." A parent's harshness can heighten a child's anger problem.

Parents can add to a child's frustration by being too structured or not structured enough. Increasing structure may mean that you warn your children a little ahead of time before you expect them to make changes. It's helpful, for example, to announce departure times in advance. It's good to stop at times and, in a sense, check the pulse of each family member. Do we need to be a bit more structured or do we need to loosen up a little?

Having unrealistic expectations can also cause unnecessary frustration in children. They begin to feel helpless or hopeless or feel like they have no control. Sometimes it's helpful to just step back and ask, "Am I expecting too much?" Unrealistic expectations can cause undue frustration and anger on the part of a child and can be a primary cause of bitterness and resentment.

Parents can help children by modeling appropriate responses to anger. Children sometimes think that they are the only ones who feel frustration. Being more transparent about your own feelings will help your children deal with theirs. You may say, "Boy, I'm really frustrated that I can't find my keys," or "I need to be alone for a few minutes to settle down; then let's talk about this some more." Children need to see adults experience frustration and respond in healthy ways.

The secret to keeping relationships open is to have a plan for anger. Anger is like a virus. It's contagious. It's crippling, but there is a cure. The younger the patient, the easier the cure. If you can help your children understand what they're experiencing and choose to make adjustments, they can live more peaceful lives. You'll be giving them a gift that will last forever.

The solution, first of all, is to partner with your children. Work on anger as a family. Your humility and teachable spirit will show your children a lot. They will see spiritual growth modeled.

Growth doesn't happen overnight. It takes time. Consistent work, prayer and self-awareness will give you the tools to get your anger under control. As you implement a plan for anger management in your family, you will see relationships open up and individuals grow closer together. Your children will learn healthy personal habits and constructive communication skills.

Anger decreases productivity and peace. It decreases the ability to enjoy life. Unfortunately, most families don't deal with anger directly. If you can help your children grow in anger management, you'll be giving them a very valuable gift.

An Anger Management Plan

1. *Effective parents teach their children frustration management, anger control, rage reduction and releasing bitterness.*

2. *Identifying the cues that a child is getting angry is the first step in helping children deal with their anger.*

3. *Stepping back gives the child time to acknowledge that anger is developing and decide what course of action to take next. Stepping back may mean engaging in another activity or leaving the situation temporarily. It may just mean pausing for a moment and taking a deep breath.*

4. *The child can learn to choose a different response. No matter what stage the anger is in, the child has several healthy alternatives which will lessen or remove the anger.*

5. *Rage needs to be controlled, not vented.*

6. *Children do not grow out of bitterness, they grow into it. The solution to bitterness is forgiveness.*

Secret Six

The Secret To Persevering And Being Consistent

"Get back into bed, Danny," Marlene called as she heard him tiptoe down the stairs.

"I want a drink of water," he replied sheepishly.

"Get a drink and then get back into bed."

Danny went into the bathroom and got a drink of water.

Then, passing the living room again, he peeked in and asked, "What are you doing?"

"I'm reading. You should be in bed," Marlene answered feeling a little irritated.

"I'm not tired."

"Look, you're going to have to get up early in the morning. You can sit here for a few minutes with me; then I want you to go to bed, okay?"

"Okay," Danny promised.

Marlene didn't really want Danny up but she was tired. She didn't have the energy to get up and put him in bed again. It seemed like this happened every night. Last night she went in and laid down with him. He stayed in bed, but she ended up falling

asleep. "I wish four-year-olds could go to bed by themselves," she thought.

"Hi, Honey," Craig called as he came in the front
door, returning from a meeting.

"Hi, Craig."

"Hi, Dad," said Danny, to his dad's surprise.

"What are you doing up? I thought I said 'Good
night' to you before I left."

"I'm not tired."

"Well, it's late. You need to head to bed."

"Your dad's right," Marlene agreed feeling frustrated. "You go in and get into bed. You had a busy
day today."

"Can't I stay up a little longer?"

"No, you need to go to bed now. Come on." Marlene took Danny by the hand and led him to his room.

"I don't want you to get up again," Marlene said
firmly as she walked out the door.

Craig turned to Marlene as she came into the
kitchen. "It's pretty late for Danny to be up."

"I know. I put him to bed at 7:30 but he kept
getting up. I'm tired. I didn't want to fight about it. I
just wanted to relax a little before my mother stops
by."

"Your mother's coming over?" Craig asked as he
dished out some ice cream.

"She has some more clothes for the kids."

Marlene's mother, Shirley, lived nearby and often helped out with the children. Marlene enjoyed
their relationship and benefited from her mother's

support and encouragement.

"Mom," Danny called from the bedroom. Frustrated, Marlene headed back upstairs just as her mom was coming in the front door.

"Come on in, Mother. I'll be right back."

One more time Marlene told Danny to stop calling and to go to sleep. Then she joined her mother and Craig in the kitchen.

"My friend from work gave me these clothes and I thought they might fit Jennifer," Shirley began.

"Thanks," said Marlene. "Those clothes you got for Danny were just the right size. I'll have Jennifer try these on tomorrow."

"How's your evening been? Is Danny okay?" Shirley asked.

"Yes, he's fine. He had trouble going to bed tonight," Marlene admitted. "He always seems to have an excuse to get himself out of bed."

"I remember that from when you and your sisters were little," Shirley said. "The list of excuses can get pretty long, can't it: a drink of water, going to the bathroom, afraid of the dark, not tired, wanting a story or a kiss or a hug." They all laughed because they knew it was true.

"Come on, Mother, we didn't do that when we were kids, did we?" Marlene asked jokingly.

"At first you did, but we had to teach you to go to bed and stay there. All children go through these kinds of experiences . . . partly because they don't want to miss out on what Mom and Dad are doing,"

Shirley said.

"So, how did you do it?" Craig asked.

"Well, I think the secret is being consistent," Shirley offered.

"It seems that every parenting book we read talks about being consistent," Marlene said. "But sometimes I just want a break when I'm tired."

"It is hard. Parenting is a never-ending job," Shirley agreed empathetically. "I remember times I was just dead tired. It's difficult to be consistent when you'd like to take the evening off."

"I'd like to be off duty once I say 'Good night,' " Marlene sighed.

Shirley smiled and thought for a moment. "As I look back on it now, I see things from a different perspective. The job of parenting is so important. Each problem you face now is an opportunity to help Jennifer and Danny learn and grow."

"It's sure easy to lose that perspective in the midst of the struggle," Craig observed.

"I guess I should have been more firm tonight," Marlene admitted. "But I just didn't feel like pushing it. It was easier to let him stay up a little longer."

Shirley agreed. "I know what you're saying, but in the long run I think you're making your job harder and confusing Danny."

"What do you mean?"

"Well, sometimes you let him get up again, and sometimes you're firm about staying in bed. Danny must think it's always worth a try to get up, and then he probably wonders why sometimes it's not okay."

Shirley paused, and then continued, "It seems that when our discipline is based on our feelings or energy level at the time, we can be rather inconsistent. One time you feel ready to discipline but another time you don't."

"I know what you're saying is right, Mother, but how can anyone be consistent all the time? There are just too many battles to fight every day," Marlene defended.

"That's true. You can't fight every battle, but you need to be consistent with the ones you do choose."

"I like the idea of choosing your battles," Craig affirmed.

Shirley thought for a minute, "One thing I've learned over the years is that consistent discipline must be based on something much more stable than how we feel at the time."

"Like what?" Craig asked, leaning back in his chair.

"I tried to focus on why I was disciplining. If I knew *why* I was doing what I was doing, it helped me to hang in there," Shirley continued.

"So what you're saying is, I need to remember why my job is important?" Marlene questioned.

"Yes, and it might be helpful to remember that training Jennifer and Danny now will have an impact for years to come. I think Danny will learn to stay in bed at night, but even more important, he will develop self-discipline and self-control."

"Hmm, that's an interesting way to look at it," Craig affirmed.

"As I think back, when I felt discouraged, or overwhelmed, I often would remind myself that God had given me this responsibility. Training you girls was my calling for that time in my life. Focusing on what's most important was a good motivation to press on when I felt like quitting."

"This seems like a secret that could be helpful," Marlene agreed. "What you're saying is . . . you think if I had a clearer picture of why I discipline, then it would be easier to choose my battles and fight them with consistency."

"That's something that was helpful for me, especially on those days when I felt there was so much to do and so little energy left," Shirley concluded. "Well, I've got to be going."

"This has been helpful," Craig said, as they got up from the table. "Thanks for stopping by."

"And thank you for thinking about Jennifer with these clothes," Marlene added, walking her mother to the door. "She'll be so excited."

After Shirley left, Craig and Marlene talked more about their conversation. Then Craig said, "I'm tired. Why don't we think about this some more and then talk about it tomorrow."

"Alright, let's go to bed," Marlene agreed.

That next evening, as Marlene carried a cup of tea into the living room where Craig was relaxing, she began, "You know, as I dealt with the children today I felt more motivated to discipline them."

"Why do you think that was?" Craig asked.

"I'm not sure of all the reasons why we discipline, but our conversation last night gave me a sense that day-to-day discipline is important. I was more motivated to follow through when I thought about my actions having lasting effects on the children."

"Mom," Danny interrupted, appearing at the doorway.

"Danny, you're supposed to be in bed."

"Can I stay up for awhile?"

Craig and Marlene looked at each other and smiled.

Even though it wasn't convenient, they knew they had to get Danny back into bed. They saw this situation as one piece of a larger problem. Craig and Marlene knew that they had a big job to do, but they were encouraged. Thinking about why they discipline gave them a greater motivation to persevere and be consistent.

Understanding the Secret

Secret #6 - The Secret to Persevering and Being Consistent is to Have a Clear Philosophy of Discipline.

Even when parents recognize that consistency is essential to effective discipline, most find themselves, at one time or another, too tired to take action. What parents need is a secret that will motivate them to persevere. Developing a personal philosophy of discipline can give you a foundation to energize you when the day-to-day problems seem overwhelming. Before you develop a motivational plan, however, it's important to understand a little more about the problem.

What Makes Parenting Inconsistent?

When my[*] son David was two, he loved to jump on the couch. There were times when I pretended I didn't know what he was doing because I didn't want to expend the energy needed to stop him. His behavior needed correction but sometimes I was involved in my own activity and just let it go. The irritation wasn't great enough to cause me to take action. Disciplining children can be hard work. At times, I didn't discipline David because it was inconvenient.

*Joanne

Often parents feel overwhelmed or too tired to discipline. Negative or unwanted behaviors are overlooked and allowed to continue until parents get irritated. The frustration builds until they become motivated to take action. The result is inconsistent discipline. What irritates a parent today may not seem irritating tomorrow. In order to persevere and be consistent, parents must develop a more solid motivation.

As Craig and Marlene learned, parents need something to hold on to when they're tired, discouraged, overwhelmed or simply busy with the demands of life. The secret to persevering and being consistent is to have a clear philosophy of discipline.

Parents often burn out because they don't know why they are parenting. In fact, some burn out on a daily basis. Once you understand this secret, you can reverse the trend of burnout and use this secret to strengthen your family. It will allow love to be your motivation, rather than anger. And your children will know what to expect so they will feel loved and secure.

I'm[*] a runner. I jog two to three times a week. We have a lake near our home and it's a great place to run. Running has a lot of benefits. But there are days when I don't feel like getting out there and running. Some days I feel I have too much to do. Other days I just don't have the energy. Some days the weather isn't very inviting. Other days I just don't feel up to it.

---

[*]Joanne

Running and parenting have a number of similarities. One day I received an advertisement in the mail that read, "For most people, the hardest thing about exercising is . . . sticking with it." The same thing could be said about parenting. Persevering and being consistent are hard work.

I've learned four success principles for running which also apply to parenting. As you think about parenting, imagine yourself a runner. These principles keep me running—and keep me disciplining—when I feel like quitting. They keep me going when I'm running and they motivate me to take action when I feel too tired or preoccupied to discipline my children. These principles make up what I call my philosophy of discipline. After you read mine, take time to think about, and write down, your own philosophy. Your principles may be the same as mine, or they may be different. Either way, you'll want to personalize them for yourself.

Principle #1: Focus on the Goal

When I go out running, I focus on a goal. My goal is to run around the lake two times, that's about two and a quarter miles. I know that's what I want to accomplish. It's not a time for me to chat with people or fish in the lake. I'm a runner. I'm running and my goal is clear.

You may develop a number of goals for your children over the years, but a child's primary job is to learn to obey. It's helpful for you as a parent to focus on the goal—realize that your children's primary job is to learn obedience. There are a whole lot of other things that can get parents sidetracked, but teaching obedience is the goal. Ephesians 6:1 instructs, "Children, obey your parents in the Lord for this is right." The Bible teaches that children need to learn to obey. Parents are the teachers. Each small act of defiance or disobedience is an opportunity to teach this important character quality.

What does it mean to obey? Obedience has a number of components. First, to obey means to submit. Children need to obey even when they think they have a better way or they don't like what their parents are telling them. It's not their responsibility to critique the parenting they receive, but to respond humbly.

Certainly children need to learn to take a stand for their convictions. Some parents hesitate to teach obedience lest they squelch their child's initiative or independence. Children should primarily learn to stand for convictions with their peers and learn submission to authority from their parents. There will come a time when children will critique the requests and instructions of authority. However, a prerequisite to taking a stand is a healthy sense of submission and honor. Parents need to lovingly teach their children how to obey so that those children can, at some point, humbly express their convictions to those in authority.

Obeying also involves maintaining a good attitude while submitting. Parents must teach their children that if the attitude isn't right, then obedience isn't complete.

Obeying is a child's God-given responsibility. It is a way of showing honor. The fifth commandment says, "Honor your father and your mother." The job of parents is to help children learn to show honor, which includes deferring to the parent's authority and obeying instructions. Honoring and obeying don't come naturally; they need to be taught.

I[*] was praising my son, Joshua (age 12 at the time), to a friend for his obedience and responsiveness. My friend said to Josh, "It sounds like you're going to grow up to be an old man."

Laughing, I turned to Josh and said, "Do you know why he said that?"

"Yes," Josh replied. "It comes from that Bible verse that says if you honor your father and mother you will live long on the earth."

Children are blessed when they learn obedience. Parents need to view each act of disobedience as an important teaching opportunity. When you understand this truth you will be more motivated to discipline consistently, even when you don't feel you have the energy.

Principle #2: Endure the Pain

When I[°] run, my calves ache! Sometimes my chest or my ankles hurt too. There is pain involved in run-

---

[*]Scott   [°]Joanne

ning. I need to persevere even though there's resistance.

Parenting is just like that. If you are going to be successful in discipline, be prepared for resistance. Hebrews 12:11 says, "No discipline seems pleasant at the time, but painful. Later on, however, it produces a harvest of righteousness and peace for those who have been trained by it."

Parents shouldn't be surprised by resistance. Yet, haven't you ever disciplined your child, and then wondered if you did the right thing because of a poor response? Do you second-guess yourself when your children respond negatively?

It's as if parents expect their child to say, "Thanks, Dad, for sending me to my room. I really appreciate the limits you set for me," or "I appreciate it, Mom, when you make me clean up my toys and make my bed." Children are not going to naturally respond that way. Those who expect their children to appreciate their discipline are frustrated parents.

When you send your son to his room and he stomps all the way there and then slams the door, you now have two problems, the original offense and the bad attitude.

Children need to learn to accept and respond graciously to correction, but this doesn't come naturally. It develops over time as your children mature and as you work with them on their attitude and the condition of their heart. The time spent talking to your children about their attitudes has lasting implications.

They need to learn how to respond humbly and graciously to correction.

When children respond negatively, it is important to look beyond the immediate struggle and focus on the future good. Remember that a child's immediate response is not an indicator of the effectiveness of the discipline. Parents must see they are disciplining for the long-term benefits. Remembering this can help you to persevere.

Resistance should not keep us from our goal. Just because my calves hurt when I run, that's no reason to give up. And when children respond negatively to discipline, that's no reason to quit.

Part of teaching obedience is teaching children a correct response to instruction and correction. Here are some proverbs you can share with your children.

> *Proverbs 12:1 "Whoever loves discipline loves knowledge, but he who hates correction is stupid."*

> *Proverbs 15:5 "A fool spurns his father's discipline, but whoever heeds correction shows prudence."*

> *Proverbs 15:31 "He who listens to a life-giving rebuke will be at home among the wise."*

Children don't naturally appreciate discipline and will usually respond negatively, at least when they are young. As your children grow, though, they will be able to develop a mature attitude toward correction. A wise person knows that discipline is valuable and that correction is something to be appreciated.

When your children resist discipline, you'll be motivated to persevere if you remember that you are working for a greater good: building character in your children. Don't be surprised or discouraged by a negative response. Work to teach them to appreciate correction but don't let their lack of responsiveness deter you from your job. Teaching a humble response to correction takes time.

Principle #3: Look for Ways to Make It Positive

When I* run, I always take my personal cassette player with me. I listen to praise music or a great book on tape. I look for ways to make the experience more enjoyable. Making the experience positive helps me to persevere.

Discipline works the same way. Ephesians 6:4 says, "Fathers, do not exasperate your children; instead, bring them up in the training and instruction of the Lord." The first part of the verse describes a negative way of relating to children. Exasperate gives the impression of being harsh and causing discouragement. In place of that negative response, fathers are instructed to do something positive, to bring their children up in the training and instruction of the Lord. Discipline times are training times. They involve teaching. Parents should not discipline their children

---

*Joanne

merely to get rid of negative behaviors. The parent's job is to train children and show them the positive direction they are to go.

You're probably saying, "Yes, I know discipline is supposed to be positive, but how can I be positive when my kids are doing the wrong thing?"

First, state rules and requests in positive terms whenever possible. Instead of saying "Don't shout," you might say, "We talk quietly in the store." Clearly stating or restating the rule in positive terms gives the child a clear picture of what is expected and keeps your interaction on a positive note. This simple adjustment can help you as a parent focus on what you want instead of what you don't want.

Instead of complaining about the clothes all over your daughter's room, you might say, "Remember, we put our clothes in the hamper when we take them off." You want to give gentle, positive reminders to point children in the right direction. Instead of saying, "Stop banging that drum," you might say, "You may play that drum outside or in your room." In this way, you are giving a choice of two positive options and focusing on a solution instead of complaining about a problem.

Another way to keep a positive atmosphere while disciplining is to look for approximately right behavior and affirm it. Don't wait until things are absolutely right. If you ask your child to clean up the toys but find that only two things are put away and six are left out, you might say, "Oh, I see you put the blocks away, that's great! And I like the way you lined up your trucks. Now let me see you put the balls in the box where they belong." In this way you encourage steps in the right direction.

When my* son, Timothy, was learning to dress himself, we had a rule that he needed to be dressed before coming to the breakfast table. When he came downstairs with his shirt on backwards and his shoes missing, we still praised him. He was trying. Pointing out his shortcomings would have been discouraging. He had tried and was feeling good. We wanted to encourage his efforts. Look for ways to affirm approximately right behavior whenever possible.

Positive reinforcement is much more powerful than negative reinforcement. Proverbs 16:24 says, "Pleasant words are a honeycomb, sweet to the soul and healing to the bones." Dish out praise in large portions, especially when you see a positive action that is a result of previous discipline.

One mother wore a golf clicker on her arm for a day. Every time she made a negative comment she clicked one side. Positive comments were tracked on the other. She was astonished to find that her negative comments outnumbered her positive ones eight to one.

Sometimes parents become tired and discouraged in their parenting because they feel they're being negative all the time. Make an effort to break that negative cycle and focus on the positive. Take time to interact

---

*Joanne

with your children about the things they are doing right. In this way, you will make discipline a positive experience. You will feel encouraged and motivated to continue on to be the effective parent God wants you to be.

Principle #4: Think Long-Term

I[*] don't run just to feel good every day. I run because I want to be healthy. I'm thinking about the long-term effects of regular exercise. Parents can persevere and be consistent when they think long-term. Discipline could be spelled T-I-M-E.

Proverbs 22:6 says, "Train up a child in the way he should go and when he is old he will not turn from it." You are training your children for the future. You are not simply changing your child's behavior to make your present circumstances easier. Think long-term. One of the long-term reasons children learn to obey their parents is so that they can learn to obey God. Obedience is bigger than a parenting issue. It's a God issue. Parenthood is partnership with God. Teaching Godly character provides the basis for spiritual development in a child. Things like obedience, submission and honor toward God are attitudes learned as a child and practiced throughout life.

When your daughter's ball rolls into the street and she starts to run after it, you yell, "Stop!" You don't want her to evaluate your instruction. You want her to instinctively stop at the sound of your voice.

---

[*]Joanne

This is the kind of obedience children need to develop in their lives so they will respond to God in the same way.

Parents must look long-term. You are building Godly character which provides the basis for spiritual development in your children. As you teach your children to submit, to show honor and respect, to be loving and kind, you are laying the foundation for long-term responsiveness to God.

There are many reasons why parents discipline their children. Developing your own personal philosophy of discipline will motivate you to be more consistent and to persevere in your parenting. When you're tired or you've solved too many problems already and you're faced with another challenge, your ability to persevere will depend on your philosophy of discipline. The strength of your understanding of your calling as a parent and your reasons for disciplining will give you the ability to press on when you feel you are too physically or emotionally tired. Having a clear philosophy of discipline will give you the motivation to persevere and be consistent.

A Clear Philosophy of Discipline

1. *Inconsistent discipline often results when parents feel overwhelmed or too tired.*

2. *Having a clear philosophy of discipline gives parents the motivation they need to persevere and be consistent.*

3. *Part of your philosophy of discipline may include:*

>*Focus on the goal—a child's primary job is to learn obedience.*
>
>*Endure the pain—resistance should not keep you from the goal.*
>
>*Look for ways to make it positive— break the negative cycle and focus on the good.*
>
>*Think long-term—building Godly character provides the basis for spiritual development in your child.*

Secret Seven

The Secret To Teaching Children To Learn From Life

"Mom, I'm hungry," Jennifer complained as she barged into the kitchen.

"Well, I guess I better get up and make a snack," Marlene sighed.

"Mom, where's my baseball cap?" Danny whined.

"I think I know where it is, Danny. I'll get it," Marlene said, getting up from her chair. Marlene's sister, Linda, was visiting from out of town. She and Marlene had been discussing some of the things Marlene and Craig were learning about parenting. Marlene was enjoying the conversation, but now she had to help Jennifer and Danny.

As Linda observed what was happening she began to feel a little uncomfortable. "Jennifer and Danny sure do depend on Marlene for a lot," she thought to herself. Not wanting to appear critical, she sat quietly and watched Marlene find the baseball cap and serve Jennifer a snack.

A little while later Marlene and her sister were talking again. "Having young children is demanding, isn't it?" Linda observed.

"Yes, it sure is," Marlene sighed. "It seems these two are always needing me for something."

"They do seem to bring a lot of their problems to you." Linda paused and then questioned, "Do you always solve them?"

"What do you mean?" asked Marlene.

"It just seems to me like they rely pretty heavily on you."

"Yes, I guess they do, but I'm their mother. I figure it's my job to help them."

"Helping children is important, but don't you think that sometimes they learn more from trying to solve their own problems?" Linda suggested.

"Oh, come on, they can't do that; that's why they come to me," Marlene defended.

"Are you sure? I bet Jennifer could have gotten a snack without you," Linda persisted, almost teasing.

"Maybe," Marlene said skeptically.

"And Danny's baseball cap was right where he left it. He just hadn't looked very carefully," Linda continued.

"I know, but he was frustrated and I was trying to help him," Marlene explained.

"Yes, but maybe you rescued him too soon. A little gentle encouragement might have been all he needed," Linda suggested cautiously.

Marlene thought for a moment. She realized it made her feel good when she was able to solve problems for Jennifer and Danny, but it was tiring too. "I'll have to think about that," Marlene reflected out loud.

As Marlene observed her interaction with her children the rest of the day, she noticed that they often came to her to solve their problems.

"Mom, I can't find my barrette."

"Mom, my shoelace has a knot."

"Mom, the toilet paper's gone."

"Mom, Jennifer is playing with my puzzle."

Now that Linda had mentioned it, Marlene was feeling like the children were relying on her pretty heavily to solve their problems. Many of the problems that Jennifer and Danny encountered during the day had solutions which they could discover or implement themselves. She wondered if she ought to make some changes. Marlene decided to talk about it with Craig when he got home.

"That's interesting," Craig responded as Marlene told him what she was seeing. "Do you have any ideas about what we could do differently?"

"No, not exactly, I was hoping you might," Marlene said.

Craig thought for a moment. "It seems that the first thing we have to do is to modify what the children say when they come to us. They've learned that all they have to do is tell us their problem and we'll solve it. If they complain about something, we try to make it better."

"Wow," said Marlene, "I don't like the way that sounds but I guess it's true. It's like we've taught them to complain about things they don't like. How can we change that?"

"At least when they bring a problem to us, they could ask graciously for help," suggested Craig. "They could say, 'Mom, could I please have a snack?' or 'Mom, could you please help me find my baseball cap?' In this way they would be taking a little responsibility for the solution and asking politely for help."

"I like that," Marlene agreed. "We could teach them that if they're just expressing a problem, they're complaining. They need to also try to offer a solution."

"So when Jennifer is hungry . . ." began Craig.

". . . I could tell her that unless she has a solution, then she's just complaining," Marlene suggested. "I could then ask her to try again."

"That's a good idea. Encouraging her to try again will help her learn a different way of communicating her problems," Craig affirmed.

"But won't the children feel like I don't care about them if I tell them I'm not going to solve their problems? It seems so cold to just tell them to go and solve it themselves," Marlene observed.

"Yes," agreed Craig. "But I think teaching them to solve their own problems is a very loving thing to do."

"You're right," smiled Marlene. "I think I'll give it a try."

The next day Marlene looked for opportunities to help her children solve their own problems. At one point Jennifer came into the kitchen and complained she was hungry. Marlene said, "Jennifer, it sounds like you're complaining. I'd like you to try that again."

Jennifer paused and then responded, "Mom, could I please have a snack?"

Marlene replied, "That was good. What would you like?"

"I don't know."

"Why don't you come up with an idea and then come back to me and try again."

Jennifer thought a minute, then asked, "Could I have an apple?"

"Okay, I think that's a good idea. Go ahead," Marlene said.

Danny couldn't find his red rubber ball and Marlene said, "I know how that feels when you lose something you want. It sure is frustrating, isn't it?"

"Could you look for it, Mom?" asked Danny.

"I'm sorry, but I can't do that right now," replied Marlene. "I'm cooking dinner. I can help you in about fifteen minutes, or maybe this is a problem you could solve for yourself. Would you like an idea?"

"Okay," Danny replied.

"Sometimes if you just sit down and think about where you had it last, you may remember," Marlene suggested. "Or you may want to go back to the places you normally play with it."

Danny thought for a minute. "I know, I'll go check in the backyard. It might be there."

Sure enough, Danny found his ball right by the back door. Marlene smiled, realizing that Danny had the satisfaction of solving his own problem.

That night when Craig got home from work, he asked Marlene how her day went with the children.

"Well," Marlene began, "I had a few chances to help Jennifer and Danny solve their own problems today."

"Really? . . . Did it work?"

"Sometimes. It sure was great when it did. But some problems aren't as easy to fix as others."

"That makes sense," Craig affirmed.

Marlene continued, "What I like about this approach is that it helps them develop a sense of responsibility for their own problems—and it teaches them to think creatively instead of just giving up."

"I think we've discovered another secret," Craig said with a smile.

Understanding the Secret

Secret #7 - The Secret to Teaching Children to Learn from Life is to Become Their Counselor or Coach.

Experience is a valuable teacher. It teaches skills like how to ride a bike, how to find lost shoes or how to pay for something at the store. Experience teaches children what it feels like to be left out, or to win or lose, or what it feels like to be put on the spot. Experience can teach character qualities like courage to try new foods, patience with a younger brother or perseverance to complete a project.

Unfortunately, though, if parents aren't careful, they can rob their children of lessons learned from experience because they love their children and don't want to see them struggle. Parents sometimes rescue their children from the consequences of their behavior and short-circuit the learning process by intervening unnecessarily.

Sometimes parents can accomplish more by doing less. That is, by helping children take responsibility for their own actions and decisions, experience can be the teacher, and the parent becomes the counselor or coach. Many parents don't realize the benefit of allowing children to experience the consequences of their actions. Wanting to spare their children frustration in life, they step in unnecessarily, but by rescuing them they may be robbing their children of an excellent way to learn.

In this chapter three discipline strategies are offered for teaching children to solve problems for themselves and learn from life.

Ask Open-Ended Questions

Open-ended questions help children learn a process for solving problems and give the responsibility for the problem back to the child. Children like to bring their problems to Mom and Dad for them to solve. Sometimes this is appropriate. In situations such as cutting an apple for a young child or helping a teenager get home from an activity, children should get help from their parents. When children are young they need to bring many of their problems to their parents because they are not yet mature enough to solve them. But as children grow older, many of the problems they bring to their parents represent opportunities to teach these children to solve their own problems.

If six-year-old Paul announces at dinner, "I don't have a fork," the temptation is for Mom to just get up and get one for him or to give him hers. A wise parent may respond by simply saying, "I see you have a problem there, Paul. What do you think you ought to do about it?" Open-ended questions encourage the child to take responsibility for solving the problem.

Some parents feel that just reflecting the problem this way isn't loving. They say, "I just couldn't do that. It doesn't seem right." Sometimes, though, the loving response is to demonstrate confidence in your children that they can solve their own problems. Parents don't have to turn their backs and walk away. Rather, a wise parent can help a child evaluate the choices, offer suggestions, and then praise the child for the accomplishment. Children grow in self-esteem as they learn to solve problems for themselves.

Paul may decide that a fork isn't necessary and then be content to use a spoon. His mom or dad could praise him for his flexibility. He may get up to get one out of the drawer only to find that all the forks are gone. Solving problems isn't easy sometimes. He may find a clean one not yet put away or choose to wash a fork that's dirty on the counter. A wise parent can offer just enough guidance to allow the child to feel the accomplishment of problem-solving.

When allowing a child to solve a problem, it's important to monitor the frustration level. A little frustration, overcome by persistence, builds determination. Too much frustration causes discouragement. Coaching the child through the problem-solving process requires patience and sensitivity.

A primary tool for helping children to solve problems for themselves is open-ended questions. Jesus was a master at guiding in this way. "Where is your husband?" he asked of the Samaritan woman at the well. "Who do people say that I am?" and "Who do you say that I am?" he asked Peter.

Here are five steps for using open-ended questions to help children solve problems for themselves.

Step #1: Ask an Open-Ended Question

"What seems to be the matter?" "What are you going to do about it?" "Why is this happening?" These are examples of open-ended questions. When children respond with "I don't know," be careful about launching into a lecture. Lectures can hinder the process of discovery.

Sometimes caring means seeing a child's frustration and taking initiative. A parent may see Billy withdraw from the other children and say, "Billy, it looks like you're having a problem. Come tell me about it." Each child handles frustration differently. Some children will come to parents to solve their problems. Others will just live with the frustration of having them unsolved. Either way, asking open-ended questions can help to move children through a problem-solving process.

Step #2: Express Empathy

If you leave out this step, children may react poorly to the process. They may view your approach as condescending or cold and respond with anger or hostility. Empathy communicates love, while at the same time allowing the child to accept responsibility for the problem.

Say things like, "I bet that feels terrible," "I understand why you're discouraged," "I'd feel bad if that happened to me," or "Your frustration makes sense."

Step #3: Get Permission to Share Alternatives

If your child has no idea how to solve the problem, you may want to offer some suggestions. Sometimes, though, people share their problems with another because they want sympathy, not solutions. Try to discern whether your child is ready to hear some possible solutions. Asking permission is an excellent way to do that. You might say "Would you like an idea?" or "Would you like to hear how other people might solve that problem?"

Step #4: List Several Alternatives

Depending on your child's responsiveness, you may want to share the worst alternatives first. As you share each alternative, help your child anticipate the consequences. After sharing a possible solution, ask, "What might happen if you do that?" or "I wonder if ____ might happen if you do that?" Anticipating consequences helps your child learn to think through each alternative carefully.

Step #5: Allow the Child to Choose a Solution

After you've given your counsel, let the child solve the problem. As much as possible, avoid solving problems for children that they can solve for themselves. When faced with available alternatives children may not want to make any choice. Life is hard. The possible solutions may all look bleak. You may ask, "What are you going to do now?" or "Which one of these choices seems like the best one for you?" Then allow the child to think about the situation. Once your children realize that the solution is up to them, they will see the need to choose.

Keep in mind that sometimes children don't want any of the solutions and therefore resort to complaining. Complaining is focusing on a problem without acknowledging or taking responsibility for the solution. Complaining is unacceptable. Don't take responsibility for a child's problem when the child just wants to focus on the negative.

One day my[*] daughter, Melissa (age nine at the time), came to me with a problem saying, "My friend wants to play with me but wants to exclude another girl that I also want to play with."

"Oh, that's sad," I said. "What are you going to do?"

After thinking for a minute, she replied, "I'm just going to tell her if she wants to play with me, then she'll have to accept the other girl too."

---

*Scott

"That sounds like it might work. Why don't you try it and let me know how it goes."

My initial thought was to tell Melissa how to solve her problem, but my use of questions enabled her to come to a good solution herself. I became the counselor.

Another afternoon both Josh and Melissa came into my office, plopped down and announced, "We're bored and it's your fault."

I was busy but their words sparked my interest, so I turned around and said, "Tell me about it."

"Well, all the other children in the neighborhood are in school. We're finished with our work. You chose to homeschool us. So, we're bored and it's your fault."

I felt like saying, "Wait just a moment," and running upstairs to get some more schoolwork, but instead I said, empathetically, "So you're bored. You wish you had something fun to do, right?"

"Yes," they agreed.

"Would you like to know how other people might solve this problem?" I asked.

"Okay," they responded.

"There are six things you can do when you're bored, besides being entertained or getting into mischief." Then I listed them. Here they are:

1. **Be Creative** - Use art, music or drama. Make a project or decorations or just think of new ways to solve a problem. Creativity can be fun, fulfilling and restful.

2. **Build Relationships** - Write a letter, talk to people, call someone on the phone, ask new questions, meet someone new.

3. Serve Others - At first, children may think this is just more work. But if they can catch a vision for pleasing others or ministering to them, then this can be a great activity. Ideas include baking cookies for the family, babysitting for some neighborhood children, or raking leaves off the neighbor's lawn.

4. Self-Improvement - Practice a skill, read a book, learn something, memorize a Bible verse, or organize your desk.

5. Rest - This is not usually high on the list but it's sometimes helpful. Boredom is often the result of being too tired to do anything on this list.

6. Unknown - God has given you a brain that has no limit to the ideas you can do when you are bored.

After listing these six possibilities, I said, "Why don't you two talk about it and let me know what you're going to do." After a brief discussion they decided to build a fort in the backyard which kept them occupied most of the afternoon.

When children run into problems, often the most efficient solution at the time is for the parent to solve it for them. But that isn't always what's best for the child. Asking open-ended questions is an excellent way to help children learn to solve their own problems. Eventually your children will learn how to ask themselves questions and they will develop confidence in problem-solving.

Natural Consequences

One of the goals parents have for their children is to help them become independent, responsible adults. The way parents discipline can prepare their children for life. Sometimes the best way to help is by doing nothing and staying out of the way, allowing a natural consequence to provide the teaching.

Natural consequences allow life to provide its own lesson without outside intervention. Life becomes the teacher and the parent becomes the counselor or coach. When a parent intentionally stays out of a problem and makes little or no comment, the child has an opportunity to learn from life.

Peter was allowed to experience a natural consequence of lack of faith when he stepped out of the boat in Matthew 14. He began to sink. Jesus, the counselor, was there to help him. Jesus also allowed Peter to make the mistake of denying him three times. No lectures or rebukes were needed—just a look from the master's eyes and Peter was overcome with remorse. Many times in the gospels, Jesus allowed life to be the teacher and he took on the role of counselor or coach.

The four-year-old who goes out to play on a hot day wearing a turtleneck learns by experience. The six-year-old who chooses to skip snack because she wants to continue her game may feel the pain later. The ten-year-old who spends all his money on one thing may wish he had not done so. Each of these experiences can be learning opportunities if the parent responds wisely.

There are four steps which make natural consequences effective.

Step #1: Talk Less

De-emphasize any instructions or warnings. Children often learn that their parents make decisions for them. By being silent, a parent may communicate confidence in the child's ability to solve the problem.

It's also helpful to just model wise behavior. You may say to an eight-year-old, "It may be cool later. I'm going to take a sweater." Or to a five-year-old, "I'm going to eat a snack now since dinner won't be for a couple of hours."

Step #2: Communicate Genuine Empathy

When the child begins to experience the natural consequence, be empathetic. You may say, "Yes, it's sad that your markers got all dried out. Those caps are important, aren't they?" Or, "Ouch, I'm sorry you stubbed your toe. I'm sure that hurts."

Step #3: Avoid Rescuing or Condemning

Avoid saying, "I told you so," which serves to emphasize guilt or condemnation. Children need freedom to make mistakes. Another mistake parents often make is to step in too quickly to relieve the consequence, thus short-circuiting the process. There's a difference between showing love by rescuing children and showing love by allowing them to learn a valuable lesson. Rescuing does teach some valuable lessons about parental love and faithfulness, but that's not the only choice. Sometimes it's best to allow a child to learn by experience. You may initially give a warning of what might happen, but then step back and allow your children to make their own choices.

Step #4: An Explanation or Debriefing May Be Helpful

After the consequence has happened, determine whether you have a teachable moment. Don't assume that because you have a desire to lecture that your child has a desire to learn. Parents can weaken the benefit of natural consequences by stepping in too quickly and forcefully. Giving a lecture takes the focus off the consequence and puts it on parental disapproval.

Natural consequences sometimes work best when the parent can keep quiet and not intervene, allowing life to be the teacher. Parents must learn to discern how much to encourage or teach in any given situation. Too many times parents believe it's their obligation to step in and point out the error. With natural consequences, parents realize that they don't have to speak in order for learning to take place.

WARNING: Natural consequences should be discontinued when property is in danger, the child may get hurt or hurt others, or when undue frustration may result in discouragement. Furthermore, if the child is not learning from the natural consequence, then use another technique. In these situations you may choose to use a logical consequence instead. A parent may hope that ten-year-old George will grow tired of a messy room and develop a desire to keep it clean. The parent is hoping that the natural consequence will motivate neatness. Unfortunately, though, George may not change. The parent then may need to choose a different approach.

Logical Consequences

Logical consequences permit children to learn about the real world through simulated consequences. They can be used in place of natural consequences to prevent people or property from being damaged and/or to speed up the process.

Whereas natural consequences simply require that the parent get out of the way, logical consequences often require thoughtfulness and preplanning. When choosing a logical consequence, first ask, "What might eventually happen if this behavior were allowed to continue?" The natural consequence of leaving a bike out in the rain would be that the bike would rust and eventually would become inoperable. Because that process would take years, a logical consequence may be applied which would speed up the process. The end result of a rusted bike is that the child wouldn't be able to ride it, so a parent may say, "Amy, if you leave your bike out, you won't be allowed to ride it tomorrow." This is a logical consequence which speeds up the natural consequence in order to teach Amy that when she doesn't take care of her bike, she'll eventually lose the privilege of riding it.

When six-year-old Tommy is fighting with a neighbor friend, it's unwise to allow one of them to get hurt (the natural consequence) so the parent may resort to a logical consequence by saying, "Since you're unable to play in a loving way with Michael, you're going to have to play by yourself for the afternoon." The natural consequence of fighting is eventually losing your friends. The logical consequence is to lose your friend for the afternoon.

Logical consequences relate somehow to the offense. They teach children that their choices have results. Parents help children understand life by simulating the real world. You'll want to develop the logical consequence ahead of time, before you actually need to deliver it. In fact, it's helpful to warn your children, just once, what will happen if they continue on their present course. "You need to be more gentle with that book, or else you'll have to put it back on the shelf." Then, if the child continues, deliver the logical consequence in a matter-of-fact manner, without anger or a lecture. You want to communicate that this is the logical result of the child's actions. As with natural consequences, empathy is essential. The parent remains the counselor or coach.

Logical consequences are illustrated in the Scriptures in a number of different contexts. In Matthew 18 the master chose to forgive the debt, but then decided to reinstate it when the debtor was unforgiving to another. The consequence logically related to the offense. In church discipline, separation or excommunication is a logical consequence because it illustrates the separation that takes place in fellowship between a person and God when one sins.

By using open-ended questions, natural consequences and logical consequences, parents can allow children to learn from life. These discipline approaches sometimes take more patience or planning but they are well worth the extra effort. If you add these methods to your discipline toolbox, you will enhance your parenting and your children will learn practical lessons from life. You will become their counselor or coach.

Being a Counselor or Coach

1. Parents can sometimes accomplish more by doing less. That is, by helping children take responsibility for their own actions and decisions, experience can be the teacher, and the parent becomes the counselor or coach.

2. Children grow in self-esteem as they learn to solve problems for themselves.

3. A little frustration, overcome by persistence, builds determination. Too much frustration causes discouragement. Coaching the child through the problem-solving process requires patience and sensitivity.

4. Open-ended questions help children learn a process for solving problems and give the responsibility for the problem back to the child.

5. Natural consequences allow the child to learn from life as the parent intentionally stays out of the problem and makes little or no comment.

6. Logical consequences permit children to learn about the real world through simulated consequences. They can be used in place of natural consequences to prevent people or property from being damaged and/or to speed up the process.

Secret Eight

The Secret To Helping Children Make Lasting Changes

"I wish we could do something about the mess Jennifer and Danny leave around the house," Marlene grumbled as she walked into the living room where Craig was reading the paper.

"You sound frustrated," Craig observed, looking up for a minute.

Marlene was tired of the mess. "Jennifer and Danny leave their toys all over. Game parts get mixed up; puzzle pieces get lost. I go from room to room finding pieces of toys and games that they've played with and not put away. I have to step over coats and shoes. If I didn't keep picking up after them, by the end of the day there'd be no room to walk . . ."

"Alright, alright, I'm getting the picture," Craig interrupted with a smile. "Why don't I help pick up around here while you finish getting dinner ready."

"Okay, you can start in the bathroom. I keep trying to get them to clean up after themselves but that bathroom always seems to be a mess," Marlene complained.

Craig spent some time cleaning the bathroom and picking up around the house. Then he went into the kitchen to help there. He and Marlene had invited the Wongs over for dinner.

"I'm looking forward to seeing the Wongs tonight," said Craig as he started to set the table. "They're a great couple."

"Yes, it's nice to see a couple who've been married for awhile like the Wongs. They've raised their children and seem to have done alright," continued Marlene as she checked the casserole in the oven.

"Their boys are committed to the Lord and raising families of their own," Craig added. "It will be interesting to see what secrets we can learn from them. I know several people who have gone to the Wongs for counsel and have found their parenting advice helpful."

Bill and Esther Wong attended the same church as Craig and Marlene. The four of them had talked at church many times and had been wanting to get together for dinner. After the Wongs arrived, they all enjoyed getting to know each other a little better. They discussed the church and other things that were going on in their lives.

After Bill and Esther talked with Jennifer and Danny for awhile, Esther commented, "You know, it's been a long time since our children were this age. Our boys were full of excitement too. I enjoy the energy children have. Sometimes our house seems so quiet now with just the two of us."

"You're in a completely different stage of life than we are," Marlene reflected. "Your children have grown up and moved out of the house. Most of our family life still revolves around our children."

After dinner, Craig offered to put Jennifer and Danny to bed while the others cleared the table and moved into the living room.

Once the children were settled, Craig rejoined the others. "Things sure do quiet down once they're in bed," he sighed.

"Yes, parenting is hard work," Bill affirmed. "But I'm sure you realize that if you work at it now, your effort will pay off."

"We've been working hard at it lately," Marlene admitted. "Craig and I have learned some important things about parenting the past few months."

"Is that right?" questioned Esther. "What have you been learning?"

As Craig and Marlene talked about their new discipline strategies, Bill and Esther were encouraging. Craig shared about the secret to prompt obedience and how a tight action point was helping his children learn they needed to obey quickly. They also shared about the positive conclusion and how they were using rules to teach values. It seemed that many of these insights were similar to strategies the Wongs had used.

"It sounds like you're learning a number of things that many parents never learn," Bill observed. "I like your emphasis on values and helping children address heart issues."

"We feel like we've learned a lot about parenting but there are some times when we just don't see the change we'd like. It seems as if we are not getting through," Marlene said.

"Behavior is often a symptom of what's in the heart," Bill continued. "As parents we want to help our children develop Godly character which will lead to Godly actions. Sometimes our discipline needs to focus on problems that are more deeply rooted in the heart."

"Yes," said Craig, "I know that building character is good but it's often hard to measure. We tend to focus on behavior because it's something we can see. If we try to develop character, how do we know if we're making progress?"

"That's a good question. Maybe I can clarify it with an example," Bill continued. " 'Don't lie' focuses on behavior. 'Honesty' is the character quality which focuses on the heart. We want to foster changes and develop positive attitudes on this deeper level. We then can measure growth in character by observing behavior. The behavior we see is a reflection of what is going on in the heart. With our family, we found it helpful to focus on specific character qualities as our boys were growing up."

"I don't think our children are old enough for that," Craig challenged. "I think they'd have a hard time understanding character."

Bill nodded. "It's helpful to define character qualities in practical ways that even young children can understand. Parents we've worked with have come up with some pretty good character quality definitions over the years. Do you remember any of those, Esther?"

Esther thought for a moment. "One mom, frustrated that her daughter wasn't looking at her when she was talking, defined **attentiveness** as *showing people you love them by looking at them when they say their words.* Another child was struggling with frustration when asked to wait so her mom defined **patience** as *waiting with a happy heart.* **Promptness** is *showing someone you love them by valuing their time.*"

Bill continued, "It gets to be fun after awhile. These working definitions give the child specific things to do to develop the character quality. When our son, Joseph, was learning how to play the piano we defined **perseverance** as *continuing to work hard even after you feel like quitting.* You see, perseverance doesn't begin until you feel like quitting."

"I like that," said Craig. "It reminds me of our definition of obedience. We say **obedience** is *doing what someone says, right away, without being reminded, with a good attitude.*"

"Yes, that's the right idea," said Esther. "It's helpful to express the solution in a positive way, using a character quality and a definition that's easy to understand."

"I wonder if this could apply to cleaning up the house," Craig said jokingly.

"What do you mean?" Esther asked.

"We were talking before you came about how the children often leave things around the house and don't clean up after themselves," Craig clarified.

"I can sure understand that," Esther smiled. "Children can be pretty selfish at times. That's exactly the kind of issue I think character addresses. Long-term or deeply rooted problems need a character development plan. I'm sure there's a character quality that could help with messiness."

Marlene thought for a moment. "It seems like it's just being responsible to put away the things that you got out . . . or maybe it's being loving to clean up the mess in the bathroom," she suggested.

"That seems to require thoughtfulness," Craig observed.

"There are often a number of character qualities that address a particular problem, but it's usually helpful to pick one to emphasize," Bill mentioned.

"I like the idea of thoughtfulness for the bathroom problem," Marlene agreed. "How could we define it in a way that our children could understand?"

Everyone thought for a minute; then Esther suggested, "Maybe you could say that thoughtfulness is thinking about other people."

". . . Or thoughtfulness is showing love for the next person who will use that bathroom," added Bill.

"I like that idea," affirmed Marlene. "I'm not sure

how Jennifer and Danny will respond to it though."

"Character isn't developed overnight. I'm sure you'll find other ways to teach thoughtfulness as well. The important thing is that children see the problem, understand that change is needed and know how to work on it. The Holy Spirit is able to change the hearts of our children. We need to pray for them often."

Craig and Marlene found their conversation with Bill and Esther quite helpful. As she thought about it, Marlene began to develop some more ideas for teaching thoughtfulness to her children.

The next morning Craig and Marlene talked about thoughtfulness with Jennifer and Danny. Marlene decided to put a little sign in the bathroom which read, "Did you check to see if the bathroom is ready for the next person?"

"What kinds of things do you think we should check?" asked Craig.

"To see if the toilet's flushed," suggested Danny.

"Hang up the towel when we're done and turn off the light," added Jennifer.

"That's good," affirmed Marlene. "Making sure the counter is cleaned off and things aren't on the floor. . . . Those are good ideas for being thoughtful to others. Let's try and see how we do."

Craig and Marlene were encouraged with this approach to the problem. Certainly developing character is consistent with the other things they were learning.

Understanding the Secret

Secret #8 - The Secret to Helping Children Make Lasting Changes is to Use a Character Development Plan.

Some of you I'm sure remember leaving the hospital with that first child and thinking, "Wait, are they going to let me just walk out of here with this thing? I don't know anything about babies." It's nice that children start off as babies so that parents can grow with them. Parenting is something we learn by experience.

Secret #8 is nicknamed "The Secret Weapon." Although you can use it anytime, this secret is one you can use when all else seems to have failed.

The preceding chapters have established a framework for dealing with most discipline problems and preventing many that might occur. But no matter how hard parents work at preventing problems with their children, they all, from time to time, see patterns of behavior that need to be addressed. The normal day-to-day plan for handling problems sometimes isn't enough. A concentrated effort is needed to change a deeper problem of the heart.

In Matthew 23, the Pharisees were criticized for cleaning the outside of the cup and dish but the inside was left full of greed and self-indulgence. Jesus told them to first clean the inside of the cup and dish, referring to the heart, and then the outside, the behavior, also will be clean. Parents need to work toward a changed heart, not just focus on changing behavior. Since this can seem overwhelming, it's helpful to have a reliable plan.

This chapter gives you a strategy for dealing with character qualities which will open the door for God's work in your children's hearts. Parents have a great influence on their children, but it's the Holy Spirit who changes hearts. As you work on any plan to help your children make lifestyle changes, you want to pray that God will use your teaching to mold their character. Parenting is partnership with God.

As you begin to address character issues in your children, it's helpful to approach problems from the perspective of a "parenting doctor." Any doctor follows a specific plan when addressing a problem. Parents can follow a similar six-step plan to identify, analyze and strategize for character development and behavior change. The six steps are:

1. Observation
2. Diagnosis
3. Solution
4. Treatment
5. Motivation
6. Follow-up

When you see negative patterns developing in your children, they're often a result of a root cause or a character quality deficiency. With this plan, you can identify character problems and nurture positive character qualities in your children. You can help your children make lifestyle changes, develop good habits, and build depth of character.

Observation

It isn't uncommon for a parent to experience an overwhelming sense of hopelessness in regards to family life. Sometimes a husband will come home from work to find his wife at her wit's end, completely frustrated with the children.

When you feel overwhelmed by the problems you see, the first thing to do is sort out the behavior by listing the symptoms of the problem. The task here is to identify negative behaviors. List as many facts or data as you can. It's best to take out a piece of paper and just start writing as many of the offenses as you can think of. You're not trying to make conclusions, just list the facts. Your list may look something like this:

- didn't finish homework again yesterday
- leaves room messy
- won't complete chores without being reminded
- quits a game when not winning
- hits his brother
- says, "I can't do it" instead of trying to read difficult words

Ask yourself these questions: "What is actually happening here?" "What words are being used?" "Does the problem happen at a particular time?" "Are there patterns which have developed?" "Does the problem occur with particular people?" Many times the behaviors seem to be totally independent and unrelated, but as you begin to write down the offenses, you may see them fall into patterns of behavior. Writing down the observations is a very helpful process.

Diagnosis

Once you have your list, look for groupings of negative behaviors. It may be that on second glance, you see that a number of the misbehaviors are related. Then ask "Why?" questions. Try to determine what root problems cause the behaviors you're seeing. Look for character quality deficiencies or positive character qualities that are misused. Look past behaviors to the heart. Several of the problems listed above suggest a lack of perseverance or a lack of diligence.

Sometimes it's helpful to look at negative traits as positive qualities misused. Good character qualities can be taken to an extreme and have a negative side. The organized child, if not careful, may become intolerant or inflexible in a less organized situation. A child's greatest strength can also be that child's greatest weakness.

My* son, David, is sensitive to others' needs. He is compassionate and cares for others. He seems to feel things deeply. I remember one time when he was

---

*Joanne

young, he began to cry when he saw an ambulance speeding down the road because it meant someone was hurt inside. He's very caring. Unfortunately, sometimes this sensitivity would cause David to become moody or overly emotional, pouting or crying over the least little problem. The positive quality is sensitivity but it can have a negative side of being moody or having emotional outbursts.

Timothy, on the other hand, has the ability to work hard at a task without being distracted. He focuses intensely with real determination to succeed. This quality of being persistent can be a real asset, but sometimes it showed itself as stubbornness.

In the diagnosis step, you look past behaviors to the heart. Look at character issues. The behavior you see isn't the root problem. Find the heart issue that needs to be addressed.

Solution

In the solution step, you determine the character quality which needs to be developed. Focus on the positive. Find a name for a quality that the child needs. Then define it in a way that is appropriate and easy for the child to understand. Don't take dictionary definitions, but rather use working definitions.

Remember, you're not just dealing with behavioral changes; you're building character. Words like "stop complaining" focus on behavior. "Gratefulness," on the other hand, is a character quality. A child who is having a hard time staying in bed after saying "Good night" may need to work on self-discipline when going to bed. The solution simply identifies and defines the positive quality which will cause the negative behaviors to diminish.

When my[*] son, Josh, was 12, Carrie and I wanted to prepare him for the teen years by identifying some character qualities which would make him successful. We created what we called the Teenage Challenge. We gave Josh a notebook of nine character qualities we believed would be crucial for his success as a teen. Each quality was defined in ways that he could understand, a verse was included for him to memorize, and an activity or assignment was given to allow him to practice the quality. The goal wasn't to develop those qualities in the weeks prior to his birthday, but to identify them for him so that he could spend the next several years working on them. Character quality development is very helpful for children of all ages but becomes most noticeable as children get older.

Treatment

Once the positive quality has been determined, next identify positive behaviors which would replace the negative actions. Be as specific, clear, simple and practical as possible.

A child may have a poor response when instructions are given. He may grumble, complain, or get angry when asked to do something. The parent may

---

[*]Scott

determine that the character quality needed is respectfulness or graciousness. The treatment, or plan, might teach that when an instruction is given, then the answer needs to be "Okay" with a good attitude.

When children are young they may hit, kick, bite or grab when they're trying to solve problems. You may tell them that they need to be kind to each other, but it's best to also give them specific things they can do which demonstrate kindness. Encourage them to talk about the problem, to "use words." When children are very young, parents can tell them exactly what words to use: "I don't like it when you do that!" And then teach them if that doesn't work, they should get help, rather than resorting to aggression.

In the treatment step, give specific behaviors to help define the character quality. Remember if you're working with young children, they are concrete thinkers. They need to understand what this new character quality will look like on a day-to-day basis.

The Turanskys and the Millers were at Sandy Cove Bible Conference in Maryland one year where Scott and I[*] were speaking. Soon after we arrived, David and Timothy began running down the halls and jumping on the furniture. I realized the boys needed some guidance about how to behave in this formal environment. I wanted them to learn how to be respectful and loving to others at the conference center. I sat down with them and explained that from now on we were going to "walk politely" when we walked down the halls. Then I explained to them ex-

*Joanne

actly what I meant. I told them they needed to walk slowly and quietly, next to me. The rule gave them specific, practical instructions about how to act respectfully in that situation. The treatment step gives children a clear understanding of what the new character quality looks like.

Motivation

Determining the right behavior is not enough. The goal is to help the child want to make the right choices. Developing new character qualities involves breaking old habits. Everyone can sympathize with a child who is trying to break a habit; it's not easy. A motivational system is often helpful for the development of good habits.

Positive reinforcement is most effective because it emphasizes the solution instead of the problem. In fact, receiving a parent's praise may be all the motivation that's necessary to change a particular problem once a child recognizes it and knows what to do instead. Be careful about teaching children to correct behavior just to please parents. People feel good about themselves when they do the right thing. That internal motivation can be very powerful. Encourage it whenever possible.

People occasionally ask, "Why should we reward a child for doing something they should be doing already like cleaning their room?" That's a good question and can be answered by realizing the difference between internal and external motivation.

Internal or intrinsic motivation is that inner drive to do what's right, the desire to make wise choices. We want to develop internal motivation in our children, and external motivation becomes the tool to do just that.

External or extrinsic motivation comes from the outside. Most of the consequences we've talked about in this book are external motivations, either positive or negative. Others include praise, getting paid, withholding a privilege, or having a treat. How do you know if an external motivation is good or not? The principle to remember is that external motivation is good if it builds internal motivation. So wise parents may choose to offer an external motivation, but the goal is to develop internal motivation in children.

I[*] remember that when I was a child I had a star chart for memorizing verses from the Bible. Some have argued that I was more interested in getting praised for a star than I was about learning scripture, but my parents used an external system to give me a love and appreciation for memorizing Bible verses. External motivation can help build positive or negative associations with specific behaviors and give a child an internal desire to do the right thing.

Take advantage of opportunities to affirm internal motivation in your children. When Jill puts her toys back on the shelf after playing with them, you may say to her, "I'll bet you feel pretty good when you clean up after yourself, don't you?" This reinforces the positive feeling of accomplishment and indepen-

---

[*]Scott

dence. When developing positive character qualities in your child, it's important to develop a motivational system to help them succeed.

Follow-Up

Follow through consistently with the plan. But don't expect drastic changes overnight. Many little steps are more realistic and effective in bringing about lasting change than large steps. Therefore, reinforce approximately right behavior. Don't wait for absolutely right behavior in order to offer positive reinforcement. Continue to concentrate on one particular character quality for a period of time in order to bring about the desired results.

As your child makes progress in this new character quality, continue to talk about what you see. Affirm your child when you see progress. Gently remind your child when old patterns reappear. Don't forget about this character quality you've chosen to work on. Continue to talk about it over time.

Children learn best from repetition, consistency, and positive reinforcement. Although you may see a number of character quality deficiencies in your child's life, it's best to concentrate on them one at a time to prevent the child from feeling discouraged or overwhelmed.

You may feel that progress is slow and end up asking yourself, "Am I getting anywhere?" Keep in mind that you are building a tape in your child's head. To understand the idea of building a tape, think about some of the things your parents taught you. "Turn off the lights before you leave the room." "Eat your vegetables." "Be nice to your sister." "Say excuse me." Did you heed their instructions then? Maybe not as much as they would have liked, but their words are still in your head. Parents don't always realize the impact of their words. But your children are listening and you're building a tape in their head as you lovingly and consistently prod them to action.

Pray for your children often. Pray that God will use your words to make lasting changes in their lives. You may not actually see the results as fast as you'd like, but remember that God is at work for the long term. He is in the process of changing people and molding hearts that follow after Him.

A Six-Step Plan for Character Development

1. *Observation: List all the symptoms of the problem.*

2. *Diagnosis: Determine what root problem is causing the behaviors you see.*

3. *Solution: Choose a positive character quality which needs to be developed to address this root problem. Define this character quality in a way your child can understand.*

4. *Treatment: Identify positive behaviors which would demonstrate this positive character quality.*

5. *Motivation: External motivation can be used to develop internal motivation.*

6. *Follow-Up: Continue to work on one character quality over a period of time, giving consistent, positive reinforcement.*

Eight Secrets
Conclusion

"I found one!" Timothy said excitedly as he looked under the pillow.

"I've got one too!" David joined in as he reached to the top of the piano.

Anticipation filled the air as my[*] boys searched the living room. Little chocolate eggs were hiding on window sills, behind pillows and under tables. They were found nestled in planters and in the arms of chairs. David and Timothy ran quickly from one corner of the room to the other and then out into the hallway, searching on all sides as they went.

The flurry of enthusiasm remained for several minutes, and then quieted. Were all the eggs discovered? Were there some places the boys hadn't looked? They each glanced down at their stash. What a treasure! . . . was there more?

---

*Joanne

Craig and Marlene are well on their way. They've discovered eight secrets and are building a family based on effective, Godly principles. Jennifer and Danny are growing in wisdom and character.

As you close this book, what is God telling you about your own family? You know the strengths and weaknesses represented by each member; so does God. Think about where you need to start. Remember that growth and maturity happen in small steps. What can you give to your child today? Choose to make one change today; help your child to take one small step.

Three days later, one lone chocolate egg sat perched above the closet door. I saw it every time I walked through the hall, but no one else did. It stayed there . . . waiting to be discovered.

This book reveals eight secrets. There are others yet to be discovered. Answers to your unique problem or situation are available. Take time to look around . . .

. . . Take Time to Discover the Secrets.

About the Authors...

Dr. Scott Turansky, D. Min., and his wife Carrie, have  five children, two of whom are adopted twins. Scott's work as a preschool director, pastor, counselor and dad, has given him many illustrations and practical insights into children and how to raise them. He is presently a pastor at New Covenant Evangelical Free Church in West Windsor, New Jersey. The Turanskys teach their children at home where they put many of the secrets to the test.

Joanne Miller, RN, BSN, and her husband Ed have two  children whom they teach at home. Joanne works as a pediatric nurse at the Robert Wood Johnson University Hospital in New Brunswick, New Jersey, where she helps many parents and their children understand the secrets of parenting. Ed is a pastor together with Scott at New Covenant Evangelical Free Church.

Effective Parenting is a nonprofit ministry which involves  the speaking, writing and counseling ministries of Scott Turansky and Joanne Miller. As they counsel with parents, children and families, they use a systematic approach, identifying character weaknesses, patterns of behavior and heart issues. They draw on their wealth of Bible knowledge and parenting insights to guide families to enjoy relationships more fully and to grow closer together.

To obtain a complete list of resources available from Effective Parenting or to have Scott Turansky and Joanne Miller come and present their material live, you may contact:

> **Effective Parenting**
> 76 Hopatcong Dr.
> Lawrenceville, NJ 08648-4136
> phone: 1-800-771-8334
> fax: (609) 771-8003

Eight Secrets to Highly Effective Parenting is also available on eight audio cassettes. These secrets are regularly taught in parenting classes. Dr. Scott Turansky, D. Min., and Joanne Miller, RN, BSN, have a relational style of teaching including humor, drama and many illustrations from their counseling and from their own families. Each tape teaches one secret from the book in a creative and powerful style that will have you laughing one minute and searching your heart the next. The audio cassette series is perfect for the mom or dad who spends time commuting in the car.

"The Secret to Constructive Discipline" is also available in booklet form. This secret has been especially appreciated and put into practice in hundreds of homes. These booklets make excellent gifts which provide encouragement to parents.

We'd love to hear the story of how this book has helped you. Please take a moment and write to us. And if you know any more secrets, let us know and we'll pass them on to others too.

Thank you!

Yes, I Want to Share The Secrets!

Parenting is hard work and we can all benefit from sharing ideas with one another. You're probably already thinking of someone else who would benefit from this book. If you would like to share these secrets with someone else, just fill out the following order form.

YOUR NAME

Name _____

Address _____

City _____ State _____ Zip _____

Phone _____

SHIP TO

Name _____

Address _____

City _____ State _____ Zip _____

Phone _____

Item	Quantity	Subtotal
Eight Secrets to Highly Effective Parenting - **Book** ($11.95 + $3 Shipping)		
Eight Secrets to Highly Effective Parenting - **8 Cassettes** ($29.95 + $4 Shipping)		
Eight Secrets to Highly Effective Parenting - **Book and 8 Cassettes** ($36.95 + $5 Shipping)		
The Secret to Constructive Discipline - **Booklet** (1-4 = $2.50 each + $1 Shipping) (5-9 = $1.95 each + $3 Shipping) (10+ = $1.50 each + $5 Shipping)		
NJ Residents add 6% sales tax on merchandise only - not shipping		
Total Enclosed:		

Make Checks Payable to:
Effective Parenting

Mail to:
Effective Parenting
76 Hopatcong Dr.
Lawrenceville, NJ 08648-4136

By Phone (VISA/MasterCard):
1-800-771-8334

Allow 3-4 weeks for delivery.

Yes, I Want to Share The Secrets!

Parenting is hard work and we can all benefit from sharing ideas with one another. You're probably already thinking of someone else who would benefit from this book. If you would like to share these secrets with someone else, just fill out the following order form.

YOUR NAME

Name _____

Address _____

City _____ State _____ Zip _____

Phone _____

SHIP TO

Name _____

Address _____

City _____ State _____ Zip _____

Phone _____

Item	Quantity	Subtotal
Eight Secrets to Highly Effective Parenting - **Book** *($11.95 + $3 Shipping)*		
Eight Secrets to Highly Effective Parenting - **8 Cassettes** *($29.95 + $4 Shipping)*		
Eight Secrets to Highly Effective Parenting - **Book and 8 Cassettes** *($36.95 + $5 Shipping)*		
The Secret to Constructive Discipline - **Booklet** *(1-4 = $2.50 each + $1 Shipping)* *(5-9 = $1.95 each + $3 Shipping)* *(10+ = $1.50 each + $5 Shipping)*		
NJ Residents add 6% sales tax on merchandise only - not shipping		
Total Enclosed:		

Make Checks Payable to:
Effective Parenting

Mail to:
Effective Parenting
76 Hopatcong Dr.
Lawrenceville, NJ 08648-4136

By Phone (VISA/MasterCard):
1-800-771-8334

Allow 3-4 weeks for delivery.